# 90
# HOUSES OF THE TWENTIES

## Cottages, Bungalows and Colonials

## JENS PEDERSEN

With a New Introduction by Daniel D. Reiff

DOVER PUBLICATIONS, INC.
Mineola, New York

*Copyright*

Introduction to the Dover edition Copyright © 2011 by Daniel D. Reiff
All rights reserved.

*Bibliographical Note*

This Dover edition, first published in 2011, is an unabridged republication of the fifth edition of *Practical Homes*, originally published by Jens Pedersen, St. Paul, Minnesota, in 1929. The illustrations, floor plans, and accompanying text for the house designs have been rearranged to better fit the trim size of the present volume. A new introduction by Daniel D. Reiff has been specially prepared for this edition.

*Library of Congress Cataloging-in-Publication Data*

Pedersen, Jens, 1866–1941.
 [Practical homes]
 90 houses of the twenties : cottages, bungalows, and colonials / Jens Pedersen ; with a new introduction by Daniel D. Reiff. — Dover ed.
     p. cm.
 Originally published: Practical homes. 5th ed. St. Paul, Minn. : Jens Pedersen, 1929.
 ISBN-13: 978-0-486-47886-9
 ISBN-10: 0-486-47886-6
   1. Architecture, Domestic—United States—History—20th century—Designs and plans.
I. Title. II. Title: Ninety houses of the twenties. III. Title: Cottages, bungalows, and colonials.

NA7208.P43 2011
728'.37022273—dc22
                                                                          2010041140

Manufactured in the United States by Courier Corporation
47886601
www.doverpublications.com

# Introduction to the Dover Edition

## *by Daniel D. Reiff, Ph.D.*

During the prosperous 1920s, if a middle- or upper-middle-class family wanted to have an attractive, well-designed five- to seven-room house built for themselves they had several options. One's first inclination might be to "consult an architect," though architects usually did not find it profitable to design small homes. But there were in fact a number of other choices, some quite economical, open to prospective home builders, thanks to the printed book. One of the most popular routes was to consult a catalog of house-plans published by one of the many mail-order plan companies, and order their plans and specifications for the preferred dwelling. Such catalogs, which provided a whole range of house designs to choose from, were often available at lumber yards and builders' offices; they were also advertised in popular magazines. The prospective owner could then study the many designs at leisure.

Such plan catalogs were well known and of long standing. The first mail-order plans for houses seem to be those advertised by Cleaveland, Backus and Backus in their 1856 book of house designs *Village and Farm Cottages*. Other such volumes soon followed. Books of plans were published by Cummings and Miller in 1865; in the 1870s by George Palliser and also E. C. Hussey; in the 1880s books of house designs by R. W. Shoppell, and George F. Barber became popular. Some architects of this era, in their ads for their house plan catalogs, were perfectly forthright: "Some architects plan seventeen-story buildings, I never have; but I do draw little, cheap cottages, and beautiful ones. If you want a house, which because of its beauty will be a joy forever, send for this book. Price, 50 cents."[1]

By 1898 one of the most prolific companies, the Chicago firm which became The Radford Architectural Company, was offering great numbers of appealing mail-order house plans. In the early twentieth century there were a vast number of such firms: Standard Homes Company of Washington, D.C. (beginning about 1921) and Home Builders Catalog Co., Chicago (beginning in 1926), were two of the most popular and prolific, each publishing hundreds of plans.[2] The designs provided could be for frame, for face brick (on frame construction), solid brick, or concrete dwellings.

Jens Pedersen of St. Paul, Minnesota, published his *Practical Homes* catalog of "90 designs of moderately priced homes," in 1929. His was part of this legion of mail-order plan companies catering to a national audience. Pedersen had been issuing such catalogs for several years; the 1922–23 edition of *Practical Homes* contained 55 designs. He is listed in city directories into the late 1930s.[3] (He also seems to have been linked to other publications related to building.)[4]

House plans like these in Pedersen's *Practical Homes* catalog were extremely popular. But where did he, and other such companies, get their plans? One source would have been the various building materials organizations. These organizations, to encourage homeowners and builders to use their specific product, frequently sponsored competitions for house designs, and published countless catalogs of the resulting designs (whose plans could be ordered by mail) themselves—or contributed the results quietly to house-plan companies. For example, The Association of American Portland Cement (Philadelphia) held such a competition in 1907; in a 1910 house plan catalog the Building Brick Association of America states that the plans were "a selection from more than 800 drawings submitted in a competition," and their plan catalog of 1912 drew its designs from 666 entries in a competition. Almost every building-trade organization of the day held competitions for house designs of various sizes, as mentioned in their house plan catalogs, for example: National Fire Proofing Co., Philadelphia, 1912; Hydraulic-Press Brick Co., St. Louis, 1914; American Face Brick Association, Chicago, 1920; United States Gypsum Co., Chicago, 1925; California Redwood Association, San Francisco, 1925; Weyerhaeuser

Forest Products, St. Paul, 1926. From their catalogs one could purchase low-priced plans and specifications of the houses illustrated—featuring their particular product, of course.[5]

Sometimes house-plan competitions were sponsored by newspapers, such as the *Chicago Tribune*, which held a national competition[6] for house plans in 1926, and in 1927 published a handsome volume of 99 skillfully-drawn designs, for five- and six-room houses, that could be built for about $7,500—a fairly substantial sum in those days, but affordable to middle- and upper-middle families.[7]

What is interesting to discover is that Jens Pedersen's plan business seems not to have been a large company, but rather to have been the work of one man, not a stable of designers or architects (as with Radford). Pedersen was not even an architect,[8] but rather a "civil engineer"—his occupation as listed in the 1926 St. Paul city directory. Although the title page of his catalog states that he was the "publisher and designer," the latter term might have applied only to the layout of the catalog! Besides building-supply firms design departments, where might Pedersen have obtained these attractive, and consistently presented, designs, if he did not have his own architects preparing them? A possible explanation for this is suggested by the front matter in the 1927 edition of the Chicago *Home Builders Catalog* (page 633): The editors state that the catalog was produced "by the same men who for 12 years have conducted the Architectural & Publicity Bureau—the Bureau whose plan service is used by eleven of the leading Retail Lumber Associations of America." Thus there was at least one major trade group (not just the various building supply companies themselves) that prepared and shared these house plans—and over the years could develop small house plans that were nearly perfect in style, design, and appeal. It must have been from such a group that Pedersen obtained his designs.

The 1929 *Practical Homes* is a very attractive publication. Each of the 90 house designs, from a nine-room Foursquare to a five-room "artistic bungalow," is illustrated in color; and though there are no interior views (the 1922–23 edition had two), each design has a clear floor plan for each story. These are all up-to-date, popular styles of the day. The most common, with forty examples, were one-story bungalows of various types, and "semi-bungalows" (a one-story effect, but with prominent dormer);[9] twenty-nine houses are inspired by English models ("English Cottage," "English Colonial," "English bunglow," etc.). Interestingly enough for a company in Minnesota, the next most frequent type, with ten examples, was Spanish (Southwest American) styles ("Spanish type bungalow," "Spanish Square type"); "Dutch Colonial" was represented by four designs, with a smattering of other types ("California-style bungalow," "Japanese effect bungalow,") and two duplex dwellings. The prices for plans depended of course on the size of the house; twenty-seven plans sold for $15, eighteen for $17.50, and sixteen for $20, with the remainder from $37.50 to $10.

The "plan number" given for each of the 90 illustrated designs ranges from 1 to 381; in the 1922–23 edition (with 55 designs) they ranged from 1 to 400; clearly Pedersen had a "master catalog" of at least 400 house designs he was selecting from, choosing those he felt would appeal most to his audience.[10] (Only 15 designs in this catalog are repeats from the 1922–23 issue.) He chose a good variety of attractive homes, comparable to what can be found in other catalogs of this period. A couple dozen of them are indeed very similar to designs offered by major companies of the day. For example, in perusing the 1925 Standard Homes Company catalog we can see that Pedersen's design no. 2 finds a comparable model in their home on p. 83; no. 9 on p. 76; no. 58 on p. 75; no. 104 on p. 100; no. 146 on p. 97; and no. 154 on p. 85. (Please turn to the inside back cover to view three examples.) Other parallels can be found in the huge 1927 *Home Builders Catalog*[11] where Pedersen's design no. 1 has its parallel on p. 1149; no. 42 on p. 805; no. 62 on p. 650; no. 108 on p. 661; and no. 381 on p. 1033.

Now that Pedersen's handsome catalog is reprinted, hopefully homeowners and researchers will locate actual examples of dwellings built following these attractive designs.

1. Quoted in an article by C. H. Blackall, "The Wholesale Architect as an Educator," *American Architect and Building News*, Nov. 3, 1894, p. 44. As Blackall noted, "It is hardly possible to turn through the advertising papers or any magazine or newspaper of note without finding frequent advertisements of building plans."

2. The Standard Homes Company 1925 catalog, *Better Homes at Lower Cost: 101 Modern Home Standardized* (i.e., using standard length of lumber where possible, to save costs), was reprinted by Dover Publications in 1999 as *101 Classic Homes of the Twenties* (ISBN 0-486-40731-4). The listed "publisher," Harris, McHenry & Baker Co. of Elmira, N.Y., was just the lumber company, who had their name imprinted on the front of the copy used for the reprint.

3. My thanks to Hampton Smith of the Minnesota Historical Society Library, St. Paul, for providing me with a xerographic copy of this catalog, and for copies of St. Paul city directory entries (1926, 1934, 1937) citing Jens Pedersen.

    Pedersen was not the only St. Paul pattern-book publisher. Charles W. Battley's Plan Service Company issued a series of catalogs entitled *Ideal Homes* from the 1920s into the 1940s. One edition was reprinted by Dover Publications in 2010 (ISBN 0-486-47255-8).

4. Although his name does not appear on the title page, the copyright page, or the editorial page, Jens Pedersen seems to be linked to an unusual series of volumes entitled *The HoltBidders Instructions* (Minneapolis: Holtbid Service Co., 1925) in 17 parts (each about 30 pages long)—a system for accurately bidding on all manner of construction, established about 1915 by A. W. Holt. My thanks to Barbara Bezat of the Northwest Architectural Archives, University of Minnesota (which holds the volumes), for this information.

5. These trade-company house plans were spread about widely—not just in their own publications. The Home Owners Institute's *Book of a Thousand Homes* (New York: 1927) states (in their acknowledgements, p. 5) that trade organizations "which have co-operated in supplying plans include: American Face Brick Association, Portland Cement Association, Common Brick Manufacturers Association of the United States, The Curtis Companies, Hollow Building Tile Manufacturers Association, National Lumber Manufacturers Association, Associated Metal Lath Manufacturers, Long Bell Lumber Company, and Lehigh Portland Cement Company."

6. The *Tribune* competition received entries from all over the country: California, Connecticut, Florida, Illinois, Indiana, Maine, Massachusetts, Michigan, Missouri, New Jersey, New York, North Carolina, North Dakota, Ohio, Oregon, Pennsylvania, Washington, and Wisconsin. The *Tribune* book was reprinted by Dover Publications in 2008 as *Elegant Small Homes of the Twenties: 99 Designs from a Competition* (ISBN 0-486-46910-7).

7. At first glance this seems like a preposterously low amount for a house, but because of inflation, and the great rise in Americans' standard of living, the dollar in those days was obviously "worth more" than today. For example (drawing from a 1926 *National Geographic*—the year that the competition was advertised) we find that a four-door Dodge sedan cost $895 to $995; a Chrysler was $1,395 to $1,895; and a Cadillac cost $2,995. Though naturally automotive amenities are different today, multiplying by 12 gives a rough idea of current costs; thus the $7,500 house would be about $90,000 today. Only the three prize-winning designs were available in cheap mail-order plans from the *Tribune;* for all others the reader would have to write to the designing architect (whose address was included with their drawings).

8. Pedersen is not listed in the American Institute of Architects online "AIA Historical Directory of American Architects" (1857–1978), nor in Alan K. Lathrop's *Minnesota Architects: A Biographical Dictionary* (Minneapolis: University of Minnesota Press, 2010).

9. Today this type of house—a one-and-a-half-story dwelling with a transverse gable and a low-swooped roof over front porch, and one prominent roof dormer—should best be called a Stickley Bungalow, after the New York State designer who first published this type in his *The Craftsman* magazine in Feb. 1905.

10. Pedersen's catalogs seem to have a wide distribution, however: the copy used for this reprint is stamped with the name of a "real estate and financial agent" (insurance) in Victoria, British Columbia, nearly 1,500 miles to the west.

    Interestingly enough, Pedersen's own impressive six-bay house at 1865 Summit Ave., St. Paul (with porte-cochere to the left and one-story "sun room" at the right) still stands, and, with its prominent red tile roof, looks rather like three of the offerings in his 1922–23 catalog: designs 39 and 127 ("Southern California Style"), and no. 51 ("De Luxe Southern California style"). None of these are repeated in the current catalog however. My thanks to Amelia Gazlay for photographing the Pedersen house for me. His office in downtown St. Paul was in the Globe Building, a rather fancy late-nineteenth-century four-story block on West Fourth St.

11. This hefty catalog not only has 604 house designs (plus 12 summer cottages, 20 duplex dwellings, and 57 garages), but also a 492-page section on building materials and products (representing 404 manufacturers or firms, all fully indexed) and a 50-page discussion on "small home architecture" and planning. I have found a number of houses directly made from their plans; 1927 was their second edition.

**Daniel D. Reiff, Ph.D.**, is the author of *Houses from Books: Treatises, Pattern Books, and Catalogs in American Architecture, 1738–1950, A History and Guide* (Pennsylvania State University Press, 2000), which won the 2001 Historic Preservation Book Prize from the Center for Historic Preservation, Mary Washington College, Fredericksburg, Virginia.

FLOOR PLAN

## Design No. 179

ENGLISH TYPE BUNGALOW. The width across the front is 30 ft. and rear portion is 24 ft. and extreme length is 34 ft. The exterior is plain but very artistic; a basement extends under entire house. Outside walls are dipped shingles and asphalt shingles on roof. The rooms are ample size and very conveniently arranged, all conveniences have been provided.

Hot water or hot air heat can be used in this house.

Price of one complete set of Plans, Specifications and Material List...............................................**$17.50**
Additional sets, each............................. **3.00**

When ordering, state if plans are to be reversed. Kindly mail remittance with order. Plans shipped within two hours on receipt of order.

FLOOR PLAN

## Design No. 200

ENGLISH type, is 35 ft. wide in front, 28 ft. in rear and 36 ft. long. A most beautiful and artistic home, the large chimney in front with craggy yellow rock around base and doorway, stucco walls and variegated shingles on roof produce a most charming exterior. The interior is in harmony with the exterior, the exquisite arrangement and commodious rooms give an excellent opportunity for elegant furnishings. Room can be finished on second floor. All conveniences are provided for throughout.

Price of one complete set of Plans, Specifications and Material List . . . . . . . . . . . . . . . . . . . . . . . . . . . . . . . . . . . . . . . . . . . . . . . . **$22.50**

Additional sets, each . . . . . . . . . . . . . . . . . . . . . . . . . . . . . . **3.00**

When ordering, state if plans are to be reversed. Kindly mail remittance with order. Plans shipped within two hours on receipt of order.

ENGLISH COTTAGE TYPE, 30x27½, with exterior finished in the popular dipped or stained shingles. Note that the plan is nearly identical with our Design No. 14, a very popular one; but the exterior appearance is decidedly different with the Colonial entrance, windows and blinds and the exterior changed from stucco to shingles. Such adaptations to modern architectural lines have been employed as to make it quite unlike the types of architecture commonly known as English. It has the distinctive Colonial doorway and blinds. It is truly an American type, and homes of this design are being built today in most parts of America.

There is an ideal interior arrangement with **six** rooms-and breakfast nook.

SECOND FLOOR PLAN

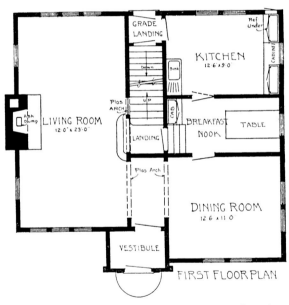

FIRST FLOOR PLAN

Price of one complete set of Plans, Specifications and Material List. . . . . . . . . . . . . . . . . . . . . . . . . . . . . . . . . . . . . . . . . . . . . **$25.00**
Additional sets, each. . . . . . . . . . . . . . . . . . . . . . . . . . . . **3.00**

If plans are desired reversed, be sure to so mention when ordering. Kindly remit with order. Plans shipped within two hours on receipt of order.

Design No. 60

FLOOR PLAN

**Design No. 175**

ENGLISH COLONIAL BUNGALOW. This house is 32x28, exclusive of sun room, a very distinctive and admirable type of a home. Its outside walls are dipped shingles with asphalt shingles on roof. Basement extends under entire house. The room arrangement is most excellent and cannot be improved upon, which a close scrutiny of plan will reveal; every convenience has been provided.

Hot air can be used advantageously in this house.

Price of one complete set of Plans, Specifications and Material List............................................................**$17.50**
Additional sets, each.................................... **3.00**
When ordering, state if plans are to be reversed. Kindly mail remittance with order. Plans shipped within two hours on receipt of order.

FLOOR PLAN

## Design No. 171

T HIS English Cottage type is 30 ft. wide in front, 26 ft. in rear and 40 ft. in extreme length. This house presents an impression of solidity and grandeur, which can be better seen by picture than by description. The broken yellow rock, large chimney in front, stucco walls and variegated shingles produce a most pleasing exterior. The room arrangement is all that could be desired, the rooms are of ample size and a tone of elegance prevails. Rooms can be finished in attic, if desired.

Hot water heat is recommended.

Price of one complete set of Plans, Specifications and Material List...............................................**$20.00**
Additional sets, each............................. **3.00**
When ordering, state if plans are to be reversed. Kindly mail remittance with order. Plans shipped within two hours on receipt of order.

ENGLISH COLONIAL. This English Colonial house, 32½x26, exclusive of sun room, is stately and beautiful. The simplicity of its lines gives it grandeur which is always admired.

The interior arrangement is made to harmonize with the design and upon close examination of the floor plans, you will find that it is beautiful, practical and convenient, and every feature has been provided for the comfort of its occupants.

The plans speak for themselves. The basement extends under the entire house including the sun room, basement walls being of poured concrete or blocks. The basement has a laundry, vegetable cellar and coal bin. A brick water table extends around the base of the house and wide rustic siding is used on the outside with green shingles on the roof.

The house is insulated between studs and second floor ceiling. The interior is birch or fir, with ivory finish.

Hot water heat is recommended, and modern plumbing fixtures should be used throughout.

SECOND FLOOR PLAN

FIRST FLOOR PLAN

Price of one complete set of Plans, Specifications and Material List.**$25.00**
Additional sets, each................................................**3.00**
When ordering, state if plans are to be reversed. Kindly mail remittance with order. Plans shipped within two hours on receipt of order.

Design No. 2

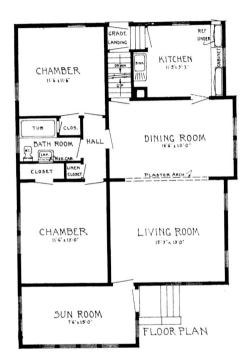

CHAMBER
11'6 x 11'6"

KITCHEN
11'3" x 9'3"

GRADE LANDING

REF UNDER

SINK

CABINET

DOWN

UP

TUB

CLOS.

BATH ROOM

HALL

DINING ROOM
19'6" x 10'0"

LAY.

MED.CAB.

CLOSET

LINEN CLOSET

PLASTER ARCH

CHAMBER
11'6" x 13'0"

LIVING ROOM
15'3" x 13'0"

SUN ROOM
7'6" x 15'0"

FLOOR PLAN

**Design No. 183**

Tʜɪs bungalow is 28x34, is a universal and popular design, its wide, white siding and green trim produce a cheerful exterior. The interior arrangement is perfect and all rooms are of good size and ample space everywhere to set furniture without appearing crowded, every up-to-date feature is provided.

Hot air heating is recommended.

Price of one complete set of Plans, Specifications and Material List . . . . . . . . . . . . . . . . . . . . . . . . . . . . . . . . . . . . . . . . . **$15.00**
Additional sets, each . . . . . . . . . . . . . . . . . . . . . . . . . . . . **3.00**

When ordering, state if plans are to be reversed. Kindly mail remittance with order. Plans shipped within two hours on receipt of order.

FLOOR PLAN

## Design No. 80

THIS English type is 30 ft. wide across the front and 26 ft. across the rear and 34 ft. long. It has a very dignified and striking appearance, the broken yellow rock at base of house and around doorway lend to enhance its beauty. The walls are stucco with variegated asphalt shingles on roof. Basement extends under entire house. The room arrangement you will note from floor plans is perfect, rooms can be finished in attic, if desired.

Either hot air or hot water heat can be used for heating.

Price of one complete set of Plans, Specifications and Material List . . . . . . . . . . . . . . . . . . . . . . . . . . . . . . . . . . . . . . . . . **$17.50**

Additional sets, each . . . . . . . . . . . . . . . . . . . . . . . . . . . . **3.00**

When ordering, state if plans are to be reversed. Kindly mail remittance with order. Plans shipped within two hours on receipt of order.

DUTCH COLONIAL. This striking modern Dutch Colonial is 34x26, exclusive of sun room. Its exterior is very attractive and the interior arrangement is both pleasing and convenient. Step into the center hall and look about a bit. On your left is a large arch opening leading to the dining room; on your right a similar arch embellishes the entrance to the large living room across which you can see the French doors leading to the sun room; across the hall directly ahead of you is the stairway. Beyond the range of your vision are the kitchen, the breakfast nook, and the second floor with its very large bed chamber and two smaller ones.

It is difficult for description to do justice to a house of this type. It must be actually visited and inspected to be fully appreciated.

The beam ceiling and built-in features may be eliminated, if desired.

SECOND FLOOR PLAN

FIRST FLOOR PLAN

Price of one complete set of Plans, Specifications and Material List. **$27.50**
Additional sets, each.................................. **3.00**
When ordering, state if plans are to be reversed. Kindly mail remittance with order. Plans shipped within two hours on receipt of order.

Design No. 1

FLOOR PLAN

CHAMBER
11'0 x 10'0

KITCHEN
10'3 x 8'0

GRADE LANDING

REF UNDER

CABINET

TUB | CLOS.

BATH ROOM | HALL

DINING ROOM
13'3 x 13'9

CLOSET | LINEN CLOS.

PLASTER ARCH

CHAMBER
11'0 x 12'0

LIVING ROOM
13'9 x 12'6

SUN ROOM
26 x 12'6

STOOP

Price of one complete set of Plans, Specifications and Material List......**$15.00**
Additional sets, each............ **3.00**
When ordering, state if plans are to be reversed. Kindly mail remittance with order. Plans shipped within two hours on receipt of order.

**Design No. 90**

ENGLISH Colonial Bungalow is 26x32, exclusive of sun room. A beautiful little home, the sun room on the side gives it that broad front effect so much desired. The walls are wood siding with asphalt shingles on roof. Basement extends under entire house. The interior arrangement is beautiful and practical; note how the sun room, living room and dining room can be thrown into one, no waste space anywhere.

Hot air heat can be used for heating.

FLOOR PLAN

## Design No. 210

THIS English Cottage type is 30 ft. wide in front, 26 ft. in rear by 34 ft. long. A very beautiful and stately home, which can be better gleamed from picture. The broken yellow stone base and carried around door entrance together with stucco walls and variegated asphalt shingles on roof produce a charming exterior. A basement extends under entire house, the floor arrangement is practical and the room sizes are amply large.

All modern features are provided, rooms can be finished in attic.

Either hot water or hot air can be used for heating this house.

Price of one complete set of Plans, Specifications and Material List . . . . . . . . . . . . . . . . . . . . . . . . . . . . . . . . . . . . . . . . . **$20.00**
Additional sets, each . . . . . . . . . . . . . . . . . . . . . . . . . . . . **3.00**
When ordering, state if plans are to be reversed. Kindly mail remittance with order. Plans shipped within two hours on receipt of order.

SEMI-BUNGALOW. This semi-bungalow is 24x26. It has the reception hall feature which so many desire. Windows may be substituted for French Doors leading to porch. Space limits our description. Study the plan.

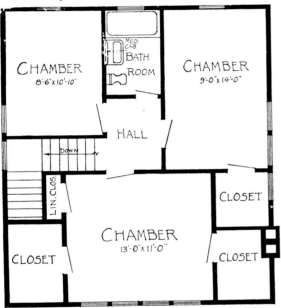

SECOND FLOOR PLAN

FIRST FLOOR PLAN

Price of one complete set of Plans, Specifications and Material List..............................................**$20.00**
Additional sets, each............................... **3.00**

When ordering, state if plans are to be reversed. Kindly mail remittance with order. Plans shipped within two hours on receipt of order.

Design No. 40

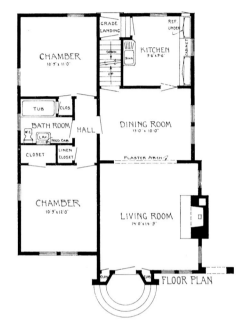

FLOOR PLAN

## Design No. 76

THIS English type bungalow is 26 ft. wide and 36 ft. extreme length. An exceptional beautiful and artistic design, which can be better seen by the above picture than by description. Basement extends under entire house. Outside walls and roof are dipped shingles, the interior is exceedingly well laid out with every convenience, it also has a large attic.

Hot air heat can be used advantageously.

Price of one complete set of Plans, Specifications and Material List..............................................$20.00

Additional sets, each............................. 3.00

When ordering, state if plans are to be reversed. Kindly mail remittance with order. Plans shipped within two hours on receipt of order.

FLOOR PLAN

## Design No. 193

THIS English type house is 30 ft. wide in front, 26 ft. in rear and 36 ft. in extreme length. The Cragley yellow stone at base of house, around doorway and in chimney together with the ivory stucco and variegated asphalt shingles on roof, produce a striking exterior appearance. The interior arrangement also is ideal, rooms are ample size and conveniently laid out with every convenience provided, which makes it an excellent home, and besides two rooms could be made in attic if desired.

Hot air heat can be used.

Price of one complete set of Plans, Specifications and Material List . . . . . . . . . . . . . . . . . . . . . . . . . . . . . . . . . . . . . . . . . . . . . . . . **$20.00**

Additional sets, each . . . . . . . . . . . . . . . . . . . . . . . . . . . . . **3.00**

When ordering, state if plans are to be reversed. Kindly mail remittance with order. Plans shipped within two hours on receipt of order.

SPANISH. This house is 32x30, exclusive of sun room. This is a sharp contrast to any other architectural design and is exceptionally beautiful when properly placed. The interior is also very unusual, but beautiful and practical. The beam ceiling and built in features may be eliminated, if desired. The picture and floor plan reveal more than can be said in words.

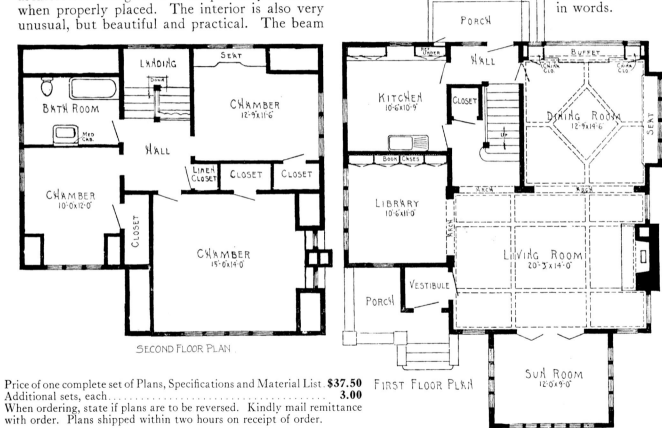

SECOND FLOOR PLAN.

FIRST FLOOR PLAN.

Price of one complete set of Plans, Specifications and Material List. **$37.50**
Additional sets, each. . . . . . . . . . . . . . . . . . . . . . . . . . . . . . . . . **3.00**
When ordering, state if plans are to be reversed. Kindly mail remittance with order. Plans shipped within two hours on receipt of order.

24

Design No. 245

FLOOR PLAN

**Design No. 83**

This English Cottage is 28x26, an ideal little home, so different from other types of homes; basement extends under entire house; exterior walls are wide rustic lap siding with dipped shingles on roof. The interior is exceedingly well arranged and handy to save steps for the housewife. Every convenience, even breakfast nook is provided.

Hot air heat is recommended.

Price of one complete set of Plans, Specifications and Material List..............................................$12.50

Additional sets, each............................. 3.00

When ordering, state if plans are to be reversed. Kindly mail remittance with order. Plans shipped within two hours on receipt of order.

FLOOR PLAN

## Design No. 205

Tʜɪs English Bungalow is 32x32, an artistic little home. The outside walls are stucco and the roof is variegated dipped shingles. The interior arrangement is most perfect, both for beautiful effect and convenience; every feature has been provided. Basement extends under entire house.

Hot water heat or hot air can be used in this house.

Price of one complete set of Plans, Specifications and Material List. . . . . . . . . . . . . . . . . . . . . . . . . . . . . . . . . . . . . . . . . . . . **$17.50**

Additional sets, each . . . . . . . . . . . . . . . . . . . . . . . . . . . . **3.00**

When ordering, state if plans are to be reversed. Kindly mail remittance with order. Plans shipped within two hours on receipt of order.

NGLISH. This house is 28x28, exclusive of sun room. It is a very unusual design but very artistic. The arrangement of the den, or library, and stairway is most unique. The large living room, sun room and the dining room adjoining it, are all conveniently placed. Beam ceilings and built-in features may be eliminated, if desired.

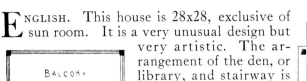

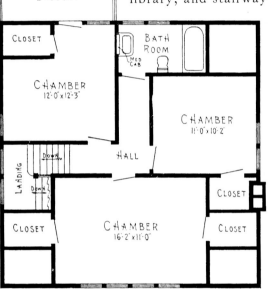

SECOND FLOOR PLAN

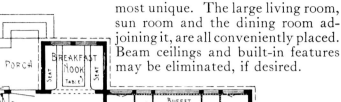

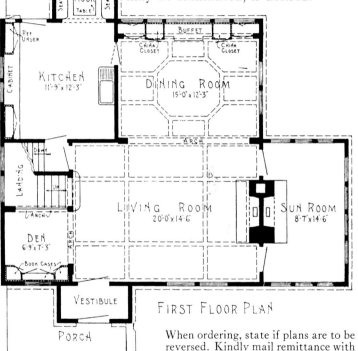

FIRST FLOOR PLAN

Price of one complete set of Plans, Specifications and Material List............................$32.50
Additional sets, each........................ 3.00

When ordering, state if plans are to be reversed. Kindly mail remittance with order. Plans shipped within two hours on receipt of order.

Design No. 35

FLOOR PLAN

**Design No. 230**

THIS quaint English type bungalow is 30x36, exclusive of sun room, is an exceedingly beautiful and artistic home and with proper setting it will be a pride to any owner. The exterior walls and roof are dipped shingles, and vestibule and chimney are stucco with timbered and broken stone effect. The interior arrangement is perfect, the living room, dining room and sun room across the front produce a beautiful effect, also note that three good sized chambers are provided, two rooms can be finished in attic, if desired. Every convenience is provided.

Hot water heat is recommended.

Price of one complete set of Plans, Specifications and Material List . . . . . . . . . . . . . . . . . . . . . . . . . . . . . . . . . . . . . . . . . . . **$20.00**
Additional sets, each . . . . . . . . . . . . . . . . . . . . . . . . . . . . . . . **3.00**
When ordering, state if plans are to be reversed. Kindly mail remittance with order. Plans shipped within two hours on receipt of order.

FLOOR PLAN

## Design No. 70

ENGLISH TYPE BUNGALOW. The size is 32 ft. across the front, 26 ft. across in rear and 36 ft. long. A very beautiful and unusual type home; basement under entire house; walls are cement stucco and variegated colored dipped shingles on roof. The interior rooms are commodious and well arranged and has no waste space, every feature has been provided for to lighten the burden of housework. Two rooms can be finished in attic if desired.

Hot water or hot air heat can be used, but if rooms are finished in attic, hot water is recommended.

Price of one complete set of Plans, Specifications and Material List.............................................**$20.00**
Additional sets, each.............................. **3.00**

When ordering, state if plans are to be reversed. Kindly mail remittance with order. Plans shipped within two hours on receipt of order.

Eいの GLISH. This house is 26x26, a strictly English design, and is very beautiful. The interior arrangement is perfect, considering the exterior dimensions of the house. It is attractive and convenient.

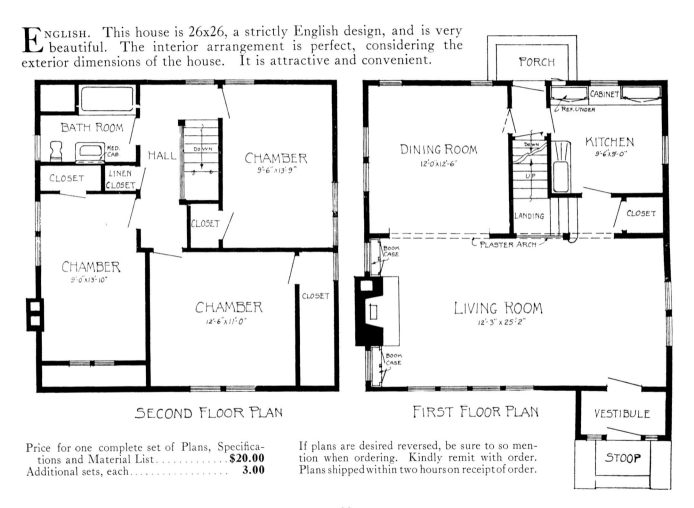

SECOND FLOOR PLAN

FIRST FLOOR PLAN

Price for one complete set of Plans, Specifications and Material List..............$20.00
Additional sets, each...................  3.00

If plans are desired reversed, be sure to so mention when ordering. Kindly remit with order. Plans shipped within two hours on receipt of order.

32

Design No. 16

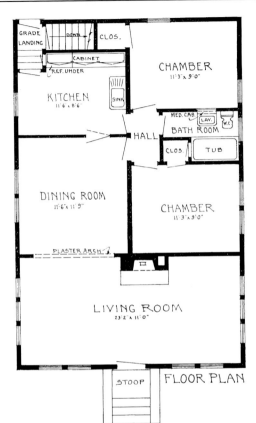

Floor plan labels:
GRADE LANDING · DOWN · CLOS.
CABINET
REF. UNDER
KITCHEN 11'6" x 8'6"
CHAMBER 11'3" x 9'0"
SINK
HALL
MED. CAB. · LAV. · W.C.
BATH ROOM
CLOS. · TUB
DINING ROOM 11'6" x 11'9"
CHAMBER 11'3" x 9'0"
PLASTER ARCH
LIVING ROOM 23'2" x 11'0"
STOOP · FLOOR PLAN

## Design No. 217

Price of one complete set of Plans, Specifications and Material
List.............................................**$15.00**
Additional sets, each.......................... **3.00**
When ordering, state if plans are to be reversed. Kindly mail
remittance with order. Plans shipped within two hours on
receipt of order.

THIS English Colonial Bungalow is 24x36, is an exceptionally cute home, nestling as it does, it creates a feeling of comfort within, which it actually does. If you will kindly scrutinize the floor plan you will find as spacious and handy a floor plan as ever devised, considering size of house. Basement under entire house, the outside walls are wide siding, asphalt shingles on roof, interior finish birch or fir with ivory or enamel finish. Every convenience is provided.

Hot air or hot water heat can be used.

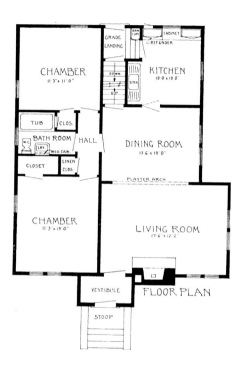

FLOOR PLAN

## Design No. 237

THIS English type of bungalow is 30 ft. across the front, 26 ft. across the rear and 34 ft. long. The broken stone effect around doorway, and in chimney adds a tone of charm to the house, this together with a light smooth cement stucco and a properly variegated roof produces a striking exterior. The interior layout is beautiful and practical as every convenience has been provided. Basement under entire house, also a large attic.

Hot air heat is recommended.

Price of one complete set of Plans, Specifications and Material List.............................................................**$15.00**
Additional sets, each............................... **3.00**
When ordering, state if plans are to be reversed. Kindly mail remittance with order. Plans shipped within two hours on receipt of order.

THIS square type house, 24x26, has proved itself admirable in all parts of the country.

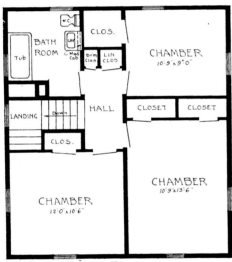

SECOND FLOOR PLAN

It is substantial, handsome and well arranged. There is an unusually good floor arrangement here, as the living room extends across the front, leaving room for a coat closet at the left of the front entrance, and a recessed hall and stairway conveniently located at the left. Note the combination stairway from both living room and kitchen, the well arranged kitchen with ample space for a wood or gas stove. There are three bed rooms on the second floor, one of very good size.

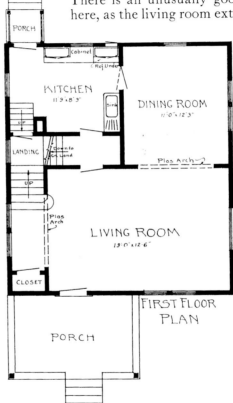

FIRST FLOOR PLAN

Price of one complete set of Plans, Specifications and Material List........................**$20.00**
Additional sets, each..................... **3.00**

If plans are desired reversed, be sure to so mention when ordering. Kindly remit with order. Plans shipped within two hours on receipt of order.

Design No. 64

FLOOR PLAN

**Design No. 165**

THIS English bungalow is 26x34, is a popular type of home. It is a design that has an eye for the future in case the family grows larger, two rooms can be finished in the attic without destroying its exterior beauty and at a very slight cost. Its exterior walls are stained shingles and brick lining above grade on foundation. The interior arrangement is handy and cheerful. Every up-to-date feature has been provided.

Hot air heat can be used.

Price of one complete set of Plans, Specifications and Material List............................................**$15.00**
Additional sets, each.............................. **3.00**
When ordering, state if plans are to be reversed. Kindly mail remittance with order. Plans shipped within two hours on receipt of order.

**Design No. 116**

FLOOR PLAN

**B**UNGALOW. This neat and attractive bungalow is 26x32. The outside walls are stucco. The interior arrangement is excellent. The rooms are all of good size and conveniently placed. All modern features have been provided. There is a basement under the entire house, and a grade entrance at rear. Can be finished in oak, birch or fir, with any finish desired.

Hot water or hot air heat can be used in this bungalow.

Price of one complete set of Plans, Specifications and Material List. . . . . . . . . . . . . . . . . . . . . . . . . . . . . . . . . . . . . . . . . . **$15.00**

Additional sets, each. . . . . . . . . . . . . . . . . . . . . . . . . . . . **3.00**

When ordering, state if plans are to be reversed. Kindly mail remittance with order. Plans shipped within two hours on receipt of order.

BEAUTIFUL English Colonial type, 30x24. This type of house is always popular, always in good demand, and probably will never go out of style. It is one of the most economical to build, as every inch of space is utilized. The wide rustic siding and brick foundation, Colonial doorway and green blinds go to make the typical Colonial appearance. A porch or sun parlor may always be added at the right or rear of the living room, should the owner desire it. This house is the smallest in size of all of the English Colonials shown in our book, but the interior shows seven rooms, well arranged and practical, and quite commodious. The center hall with stairway and large living room adjoining are features of the Colonial days.

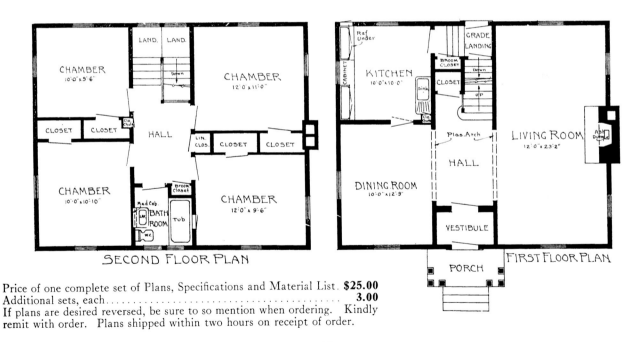

SECOND FLOOR PLAN

FIRST FLOOR PLAN

Price of one complete set of Plans, Specifications and Material List. **$25.00**
Additional sets, each . . . . . . . . . . . . . . . . . . . . . . . . . . . . . . . . . . . . . . . **3.00**
If plans are desired reversed, be sure to so mention when ordering. Kindly remit with order. Plans shipped within two hours on receipt of order.

Design No. 62

FLOOR PLAN

**Design No. 196**

THIS English Colonial Cottage type is 32 ft. across front, 24 ft. across back and 32 ft. long. These homes are always admired. Its wide white siding and green asphalt shingles on roof produce a harmonious whole. The interior arrangement could not be improved upon; there is also another important feature, if additional rooms should at any time be needed, two rooms could be finished in attic at a slight cost. Every convenience has been provided.

Hot air heat is recommended.

Price of one complete set of Plans, Specifications and Material
    List...........................................................**$15.00**
Additional sets, each................................. **3.00**
When ordering, state if plans are to be reversed. Kindly mail remittance with order. Plans shipped within two hours on receipt of order.

42

FIRST FLOOR PLAN

## Design No. 132

**D**ESIGN No. 132. Brick and stucco bungalow, 26x34, exclusive of sun room. The red brick foundation, cream stucco walls, red asphalt shingles and olive green trim make a very pleasing combination. There is not an inch of waste space in the interior. Here we have the living room, sun room and dining room in front, which is a desirable feature to many. The bedrooms are in the rear; and the kitchen, hall and bath room are in the center.

There is a nice space for a kitchen cabinet, and the refrigerator is easily reached from the rear entrance, without entering the kitchen.

Price of one complete set of Plans, Specifications and Material List. . . . . . . . . . . . . . . . . . . . . . . . . . . . . . . . . . . . . . . . . . . . . . .**$15.00**

Additional sets, each. . . . . . . . . . . . . . . . . . . . . . . . . . . . . **3.00**

When ordering, state if plans are to be reversed. Kindly mail remittance with order. Plans shipped within two hours on receipt of order.

**S**EMI-BUNGALOW. This semi-bungalow is 26x30. Its beauty is self-evident. It is a house of which the most discriminating of home owners can be proud. Some of the features are the long living room with its attractive fireplace, the combination stairway, the breakfast nook, which can be entered from either the kitchen or the dining room.

The flower boxes, when filled with bright-colored flowers, will add to the charm of the exterior. Many a restful summer evening will be spent on the large front porch.

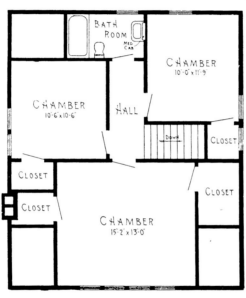

SECOND FLOOR PLAN

FIRST FLOOR PLAN

Price of one complete set of Plans, Specifications and Material List. **$25.00**
Additional sets, each . . . . . . . . . . . . . . . . . . . . . . . . . . . . . . . . . . . . . . **3.00**

When ordering, state if plans are to be reversed.  Kindly mail remittance with order.  Plans shipped within two hours on receipt of order.

Design No. 27

KITCHEN
9'-3"x10'-0"

CABINET
REF UNDER
BRM
CLOS.

GRADE
LANDING

CHAMBER
10'-6"x10'-6"

DINING ROOM
12'-3"x9'-0"

HALL

CLOS.    TUB

BATH ROOM

MED CAB    LAV    W.C.

LINEN
CLOS.    CLOSET

PLASTER ARCH

LIVING ROOM
16'-3"x11'-2"

CHAMBER
10'-6"x12'-0"

FLOOR PLAN

SUN ROOM
15'-0"x8'-0"

**Design No. 187**

THIS bungalow is 28 ft. across the front, 24 ft. in rear and 32 ft. long. The design is very popular; basement under entire house; exterior of foundation above grade is brick, narrow siding on outside walls and dipped shingles in gables and asphalt shingles on roof. The interior room arrangement is very practical and everything has been pro- vided. A large attic is also a feature of this house. Hot water or hot air heat can be used.

Price of one complete set of Plans, Specifications and Material List.........................................**$15.00**
Additional sets, each...............................**3.00**
When ordering, state if plans are to be reversed. Kindly mail remittance with order. Plans shipped within two hours on receipt of order.

CHAMBER
9'-6"x9'-2"

BATH ROOM

GRADE LANDING

LINEN CLOSET

C.MED. CAB

C REF. UNDER

KITCHEN
8'-9"x10'-6"

CLOSET

UP

HALL

CHAMBER
12'-5"x10'-6"

DINING ROOM
13'-0"x10'-6"

CLOSET

PLASTER ARCH

HALL

PLASTER ARCH

LIVING ROOM
19'-8"x12'-4"

VESTIBULE

STOOP

FLOOR PLAN

**Design No. 106**

THIS bungalow is 26x38, a very attractive and out of the ordinary design. The exterior is smooth stucco. A careful study of the floor plan will convince you of a most excellent arrangement in every particular, as up-to-date features are provided throughout.

The basement extends under entire house, with rear grade entry, also large attic with stairway from the center hall.

Price of one complete set of Plans, Specifications and Material List . . . . . . . . . . . . . . . . . . . . . . . . . . . . . . . . . . . . . . . . . . . **$15.00**
Additional sets, each . . . . . . . . . . . . . . . . . . . . . . . . . . . . . . . **3.00**
When ordering, state if plans are to be reversed. Kindly mail remittance with order. Plans shipped within two hours on receipt of order.

**D**UTCH COLONIAL. This house is 26x26, exclusive of sun room. With a proper setting, this Dutch Colonial, with red brick foundation, wide rustic siding, painted white, and green shutters and shingles, will produce a very striking appearance. A glance at the floor plan and you will observe a beautiful and practical arrangement throughout, as every convenience has been provided.

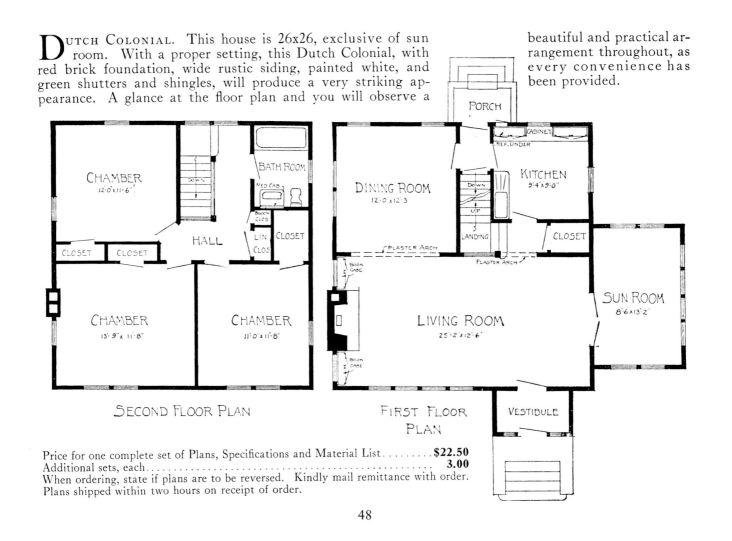

SECOND FLOOR PLAN

FIRST FLOOR PLAN

Price for one complete set of Plans, Specifications and Material List........$22.50
Additional sets, each...............................................3.00
When ordering, state if plans are to be reversed. Kindly mail remittance with order.
Plans shipped within two hours on receipt of order.

Design No. 10

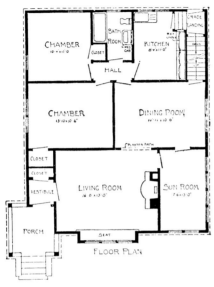

FLOOR PLAN

**Design No. 110**

THIS beautiful bungalow is 30x36. It is brick from grade to under side of windows, with smooth stucco above. The interior, with large living room, fireplace, and plastic Gothic arch between it and dining room, with French doors leading from both to sun room, produces a wonderful effect. The rear center hall leading to all rooms is another admirable feature.

Basement under entire house with rear grade entry, large attic. Every convenience is provided for.

Price of one complete set of Plans, Specifications and Material List . . . . . . . . . . . . . . . . . . . . . . . . . . . . . . . . . . . . . . . . . . . . . **$15.00**
Additional sets, each . . . . . . . . . . . . . . . . . . . . . . . . . . . . . . **3.00**

When ordering, state if plans are to be reversed. Kindly mail remittance with order. Plans shipped within two hours on receipt of order.

**Design No. 220**

THIS bungalow is 24x30. Economy has been the watch word in designing this home to meet the needs of the family with small means and still produce a house that its owner can be proud of. Basement extends under entire house. Outside walls are wood siding and asphalt shingles on roof; interior arrangement is perfect and every convenience is provided.

Hot air heat is recommended.

Price of one complete set of Plans, Specifications and Material List . . . . . . . . . . . . . . . . . . . . . . . . . . . . . . . . . . . . . . . . **$12.50**

Additional sets, each . . . . . . . . . . . . . . . . . . . . . . . . . . . . **3.00**

When ordering, state if plans are to be reversed. Kindly mail remittance with order. Plans shipped within two hours on receipt of order.

51

SQUARE TYPE. This house is 26x26, exclusive of sun room. With brick from base to window sills and panel stucco above, it produces a very attractive exterior. Every available inch of interior floor space has been utilized to the best advantage.

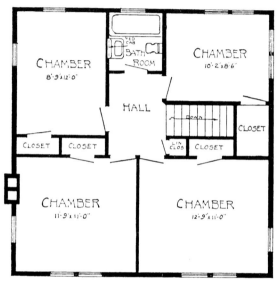

SECOND FLOOR PLAN

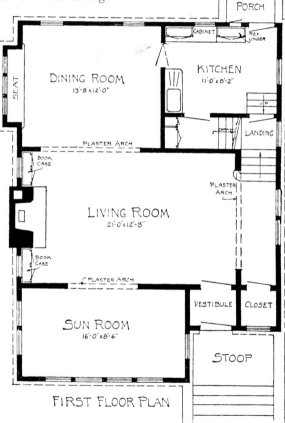

FIRST FLOOR PLAN

Price for one set of Plans, Specifications and Material List... **$25.00**
Additional sets, each.................................... **3.00**

If plans are desired reversed, be sure to so mention when ordering. Kindly remit with order. Plans shipped within two hours on receipt of order.

Design No. 24

FLOOR PLAN

**Design No. 158**

This English Colonial bungalow, 28x26, is planned to be built of frame construction with shingles (or siding) exterior, shingle roof, red brick base or water table, and brick chimney. It can be accommodated on less than a forty foot lot. There are four rooms.

It is a small bungalow, cozy, and in very good taste; its charm is due to its pleasing proportions and simple details.

Price of one complete set of Plans, Specifications and
  Material List . . . . . . . . . . . . . . . . . . . . . . . . . . . . . . . . . . **$15.00**
Additional sets, each. . . . . . . . . . . . . . . . . . . . . . . . . . . . . **3.00**
When ordering, state if plans are to be reversed. Kindly mail remittance with order. Plans shipped within two hours on receipt of order.

54

FLOOR PLAN

## Design No. 156

SEMI-BUNGALOW, 26x36. Although a small plate was made of this fine house, it is really much larger than might appear from the picture. It has five rooms on the first floor, and two rooms may be finished on the second floor, if desired. The center hallway from which all rooms and stairway to the attic may be entered is a noteworthy feature of this plan.

The exterior shows touches of the English design; the finish is ivory stucco, with brick base and red composition roof. There is a grade entry to the kitchen at the right.

Price of one complete set of Plans, Specifications and Material List . . . . . . . . . . . . . . . . . . . . . . . . . . . . . . . **$15.00**

Additional sets, each. . . . . . . . . . . . . . . . . . . . . . . . . . . . . **3.00**

When ordering, state if plans are to be reversed. Kindly mail remittance with order. Plans shipped within two hours on receipt of order.

Eⁿglish Colonial. This house is 28x28 and has true Colonial architectural lines. It has a brick foundation, wide rustic siding and green shingles on roof. Basement has laundry, vegetable room and coal bin. Hot water heat is recommended for this type of house.

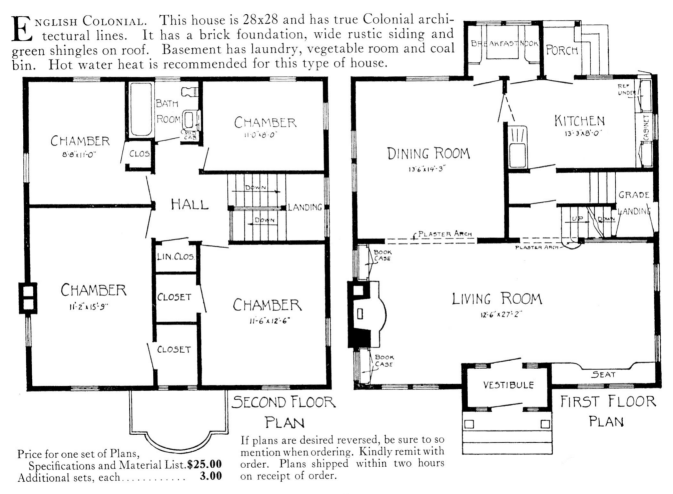

BATH ROOM
CHAMBER 8·8"x11·0"
CLOS.
CHAMBER 11·0"x8·0"
HALL
DOWN
DOWN
LANDING
LIN. CLOS.
CLOSET
CHAMBER 11·2"x15·9"
CLOSET
CHAMBER 11·6"x12·6"

SECOND FLOOR PLAN

BREAKFAST NOOK
PORCH
REF. UNDER
KITCHEN 13·3"x8·0"
CABINET
DINING ROOM 13·6"x14·3"
GRADE LANDING
UP
DOWN
PLASTER ARCH
PLASTER ARCH
BOOK CASE
LIVING ROOM 12·6"x27·2"
BOOK CASE
VESTIBULE
SEAT

FIRST FLOOR PLAN

Price for one set of Plans,
Specifications and Material List. **$25.00**
Additional sets, each............ **3.00**

If plans are desired reversed, be sure to so mention when ordering. Kindly remit with order. Plans shipped within two hours on receipt of order.

Design No. 6

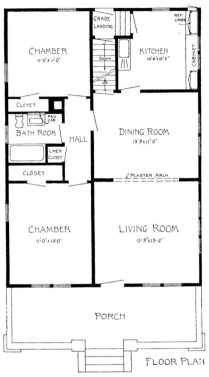

CHAMBER
11'-0"x11'-0"

KITCHEN
10'-6"x10'-2"

GRADE
LANDING

REF.
UNDER

CABINET

DOWN

UP

CLOSET

MED.
CAB.

BATH ROOM

HALL

DINING ROOM
13'-9"x11'-0"

LINEN
CLOSET

CLOSET

PLASTER ARCH.

CHAMBER
11'-0"x13'-0"

LIVING ROOM
13'-9"x13'-2"

PORCH

FLOOR PLAN

Price for one complete set of Plans,
Specifications and Material List.**$15.00**
Additional sets, each............ **3.00**
When ordering, state if plans are to be
reversed. Kindly mail remittance with
order. Plans shipped within two hours on
receipt of order.

## Design No. 118

THIS stucco bungalow is 26x36, a very beautiful and unique design. Basement under entire house, with grade entrance at rear. The interior arrangement is practical and convenient, and all available space has been utilized. Attic is also provided.

Can be finished in any woods or finish desired.

Hot water or hot air heat can be used.

This bungalow will appeal to the prospective home owners who want the maximum of comfort in a very reasonably-priced home.

FLOOR PLAN

## Design No. 160

Colonial Bungalow, 26x34. The exterior is a simple, admirable and pleasing design. Its simplicity of construction makes it economical to build. The exterior walls are covered with either dipped or stained shingles. A fireplace is provided in the plan.

The interior is well arranged with no waste space anywhere. Two rooms may be finished in the attic, if desired, as a stairway is provided. Basement extends under entire house.

Price of one complete set of Plans, Specifications and Material List............................................**$17.50**
Additional sets, each............................... **3.00**
When ordering, state if plans are to be reversed. Kindly mail remittance with order. Plans shipped within two hours on receipt of order.

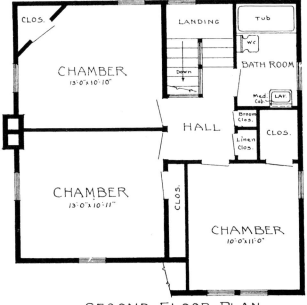

## SECOND FLOOR PLAN

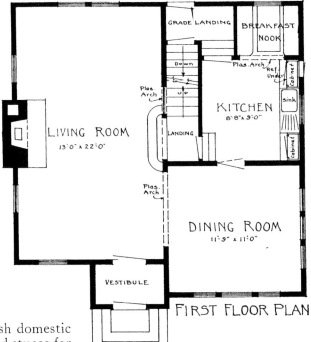

## FIRST FLOOR PLAN

A six room house, 26x26, patterned after the English domestic style of architecture. The construction is frame and stucco for the exterior finish, with half timbers in the gable ends. The sloping roof with variegated shingles, the half timber effect, the brick water table, brick steps to entrance are used to carry out the English spirit. There is a very practical arrangement of the interior, with its large living room and fireplace, dining room to the front, combination stairway from living room and kitchen. And we have three chambers on the second floor, all with ample closet space. A linen closet and broom closet have been planned. This is a desirable home.

Price for one complete set of Plans,
   Specifications and Material List...**$20.00**
Additional sets, each............... **3.00**
When ordering, state if plans are to be reversed. Kindly mail remittance with order. Plans shipped within two hours on receipt of order.

Design No. 44

**Design No. 146**

Colonial Bungalow, 32x28. In this design, Colonial refinement and practical qualities have been carefully blended with the result of an attractive small home bungalow that is very moderate in building cost. When completed with the white clapboards, green shutters and the blue, black and green variegated shingles on the roof, there is a most harmonizing exterior and a delightful home. There is a practical room arrangement, and at the same time a departure from the ordinary. Note the large living room. There is a large attic which can be used as a playroom, or for storage purposes. The basement extends under entire house. Hot water or hot air heat may be used.

## Design No. 138

**D**ESIGN No. 138. The Spanish Type Bungalow here shown is 26x38, exclusive of sun room, and is particularly adaptable to a corner lot. It is of the Southern California Spanish architecture so popular today. The rich red tile roof, the ornamental iron work, and the red brick foundation produce a characteristic effect. The doorway is really beautiful and inviting. The living room, 13'3" by 17'6" is of good size and pleasant. The large fireplace, the French doors to the sun parlor and wide archway to the dining room gives an opportunity here for careful study in furnishings, as a remarkably beautiful interior decoration might be planned. A floor of tile, dark red, black, white or variegated, would be quite appropriate in sun room. This house will give any owner a thrill of joy and satisfaction.

Price of one complete set of Plans, Specifications and
    Material List..................................**$17.50**
Additional sets, each.............................. **3.00**
When ordering, state if plans are to be reversed. Kindly mail remittance with order. Plans shipped within two hours on receipt of order.

**S**EMI-BUNGALOW.
This semi-bunga-
low is 28½x28. People
who favor the semi-
bungalow style of
dwelling will
find it inter-
esting to
study closely
the perfectly
arranged in-
terior of this
home.

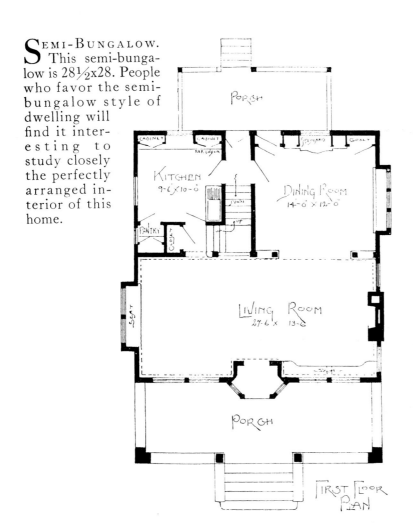

Porch

Kitchen
9-6' X 10-0

Cabinet
Ref. Ladder

Cabinet

Cupboard

Closet

Dining Room
14-0' X 12-0

Pantry

Closet

Down

Up

Seat

Living Room
27-6' X 13-0

Porch

First Floor Plan

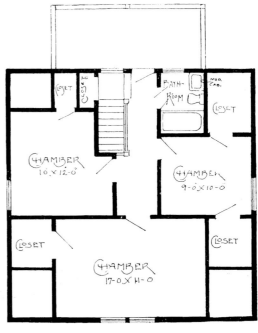

Closet

Closet

Bath-Room

Med. Cab.

Closet

Chamber
16' X 12-0

Chamber
9-0' X 10-0

Closet

Closet

Chamber
17-0 X 14-0

## SECOND FLOOR PLAN

Price of one complete set of Plans, Specifications and
    Material List......................**$22.50**
Additional sets, each.................... **3.00**

When ordering, state if plans are to be reversed.
Kindly mail remittance with order. Plans shipped
within two hours on receipt of order.

Design No. 47

FLOOR PLAN

**Design No. 134**

D ESIGN No. 134. Spanish design, 30 feet across front, 26 feet wide in rear, and total length is 34 ft. A decided departure from all of the others, it is the only Spanish Bungalow we are showing with the chimney in front alongside the front entrance. The full length doors, the small brick terrace with the wrought iron railing in front make the design characteristic of the Italian style, and certainly gives it a note of distinction. The outside walls have the rough stucco, with brick trimming; the roof is the red asphalt or composition shingle. The interior rooms are well arranged, the two chambers and bath room being all connected through a hallway. Stairs are provided to the second floor where a room may be finished off, if desired.

Price of one complete set of Plans, Specifications and
    Material List. . . . . . . . . . . . . . . . . . . . . . . . . . . . . . . . . .**$15.00**
Additional sets, each. . . . . . . . . . . . . . . . . . . . . . . . . . . . . **3.00**
When ordering, state if plans are to be reversed. Kindly mail remittance with order. Plans shipped within two hours on receipt of order.

FLOOR PLAN

## Design No. 152

Bungalow, 24x36. This bungalow will meet with general approval everywhere. It is more than just "four walls and a roof," as are so many of the bungalows of this size.

The exterior walls are covered with four-inch siding; roof covering may be composition or shingles. There is a concrete block foundation and cellar is excavated under entire house. The pro-jection on the side makes a pleasing break in the outside wall, and adds more space to the dining room.

Price of one complete set of Plans, Specifications and
    Material List.................................**$15.00**
Additional sets, each.............................. **3.00**
When ordering, state if plans are to be reversed. Kindly mail remittance with order. Plans shipped within two hours on receipt of order.

Design No. 58. This two-story square type house is 24x26, always staple and practicable; it is, of course, a very economical house to construct. The special features of the interior are the large living room, combination stairs from both living room and kitchen, and side grade entry to basement and to hall. Chimney goes through the kitchen to accommodate a cooking stove, if desired.

The second floor provides three spacious rooms with plenty of closet space; a bath room, and center hall. All of the rooms upstairs open into the center hall. There is also a linen closet and broom closet included in the plans. There is no waste space in this house.

Hot water heat is recommended.

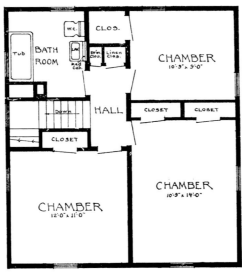

SECOND FLOOR PLAN

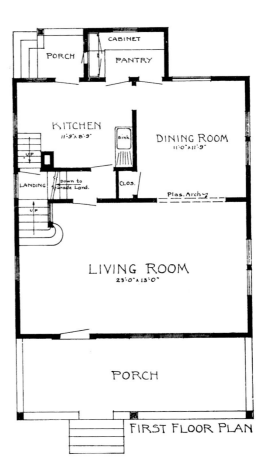

FIRST FLOOR PLAN

Price of one complete set of Plans, Specifications and Material List. **$20.00**
Additional sets, each.............................................. **3.00**
When ordering, state if plans are to be reversed.  Kindly mail remittance with order.  Plans shipped within two hours on receipt of order.

Design No. 58

FLOOR PLAN

**Design No. 144**

ENGLISH BUNGALOW, 26x36. Pride of owner-ship results from building a well designed house—one that will be a source of comfort to the owner. Here is one that can be strongly recommended as a gem in small house architecture. It has an individuality which is seldom seen in a house of this size. The archway at the right gives the house an appearance of greater width, so necessary to this style of house. There are five rooms, all correctly arranged; a fireplace adds to its attractiveness. A stairway leads to the attic storage space. The exterior should be stucco, but could be changed to shingles, if desired.

Price of one complete set of Plans, Specifications and Material List.................................................**$20.00**
Additional sets, each............................... **3.00**
When ordering, state if plans are to be reversed. Kindly mail remittance with order. Plans shipped within two hours on receipt of order.

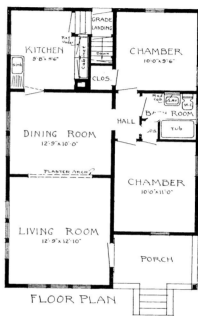

KITCHEN
9'8"x5'6"

GRADE
LANDING

Ref.
Under

Cabinet

Down

CHAMBER
10'0"x9'6"

CLOS.

DINING ROOM
12'9"x10'0"

Med
Cab

LAV.

W.C.

BATH ROOM

HALL

TUB

CLOS.

PLASTER ARCH

CHAMBER
10'0"x11'0"

LIVING ROOM
12'9"x12'10"

PORCH

FLOOR PLAN

## Design No. 124

Design No. 124. Frame bungalow, 24x34. This house is the same size as Design 122. The floor plans are exactly the same, but reversed, and the size of the rooms are the same. Note that both have the grade entrance to rear, and have attic space. This design is always staple, and if in a good location can readily be converted into cash, for it is economical to build. For an inexpensive bungalow here is a good one.

Price for one complete set of Plans, Specifications and Material List.................................................**$12.50**
Additional sets, each...............................**3.00**
When ordering, state if plans are to be reversed. Kindly mail remittance with order. Plans shipped within two hours on receipt of order.

**D**UTCH COLONIAL. This Dutch Colonial is 24x24, exclusive of sun room. It can be built on a 40 foot lot without looking crowded. It has a brick base, wide rustic siding above, and is about as economical a Dutch Colonial as can be designed. Considering the dimensions of this house, the number of rooms, and their size, is noteworthy.

The large living room is connected with sun room and dining room. The combination stairway from living room and kitchen, with grade landing and stairway under, is an admirable feature of this house. The second floor-lay-out is most convenient.

Every modern feature has been embodied in this plan.

SECOND FLOOR PLAN

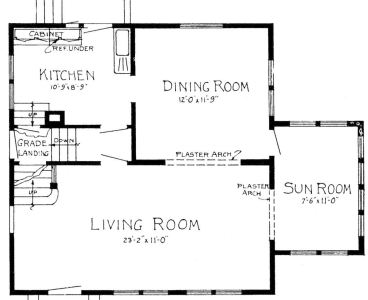

FIRST FLOOR PLAN

Price of one complete set of Plans, Specifications and
  Material List................................$20.00
Additional sets, each............................ 3.00

When ordering, state if plans are to be reversed. Kindly mail remittance with order. Plans shipped within two hours on receipt of order.

72

Design No. 12

FLOOR PLAN

**Design No. 150**

Bungalow, 24x32. This is a practical and popular bungalow very much in demand, and for the man of small means it certainly gives a most satisfactory home. It will go on a narrow lot, but the length gives rooms of fair size. The plaster arch between the living room and dining room gives the feeling of spaciousness, even though the rooms are not as large as some of the bungalows shown in this book. Two rooms may be finished in the attic, if desired. A very economical house to build, and still have every convenience. The house is entirely frame construction with concrete block foundation under entire building.

Price of one complete set of Plans, Specifications and Material List............................................**$12.50**
Additional sets, each................................. **3.00**
When ordering, state if plans are to be reversed. Kindly mail remittance with order. Plans shipped within two hours on receipt of order.

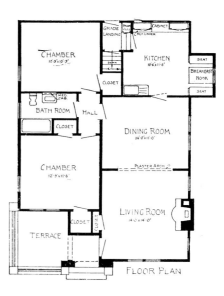

FLOOR PLAN

## Design No. 112

SPANISH BUNGALOW. This new Spanish type bungalow is 28x38, of a very artistic and unusually pretty design, fills the wants of those who desire to deviate from the ordinary. It is very striking in exterior appearance. The interior arrangement is as perfect as can be made, and nothing has been overlooked for the comfort and convenience of the occupants. The cozy breakfast nook is an attractive feature. Basement fully equipped, with grade entry at rear.

Price of one complete set of Plans, Specifications and
    Material List.................................**$17.50**
Additional sets, each.............................. **3.00**

When ordering, state if plans are to be reversed. Kindly mail remittance with order. Plans shipped within two hours on receipt of order.

ENGLISH. This house is 27½x30, a very unusual type of English design. Brick water table extends around base of house, with stucco above. The interior arrangement is practical and complete. Rooms are all good size. Another convenient feature is the combination stairway leading from living room and also from breakfast room. Nothing has been overlooked in this design to make it modern in every respect.

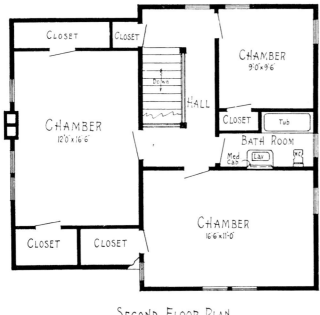

SECOND FLOOR PLAN

FIRST FLOOR PLAN

Price for one set of Plans, Specifications and Material
List..................................................$22.50
Additional sets, each.............................. 3.00

If plans are desired reversed, be sure to so mention when ordering. Kindly remit with order. Plans shipped within two hours on receipt of order.

Design No. 14

FLOOR PLAN

**Design No. 148**

T HIS neat and attractive bungalow is 24x38. The outside walls are ivory stucco with brick water table extending around the house; basement is excavated under the entire building. Note the large living room, and the ideal arrangement of the rooms. There is a grade landing at the rear, and a stairway to attic storage space. The fireplace is an added feature.

Price of one complete set of Plans, Specifications and Material
List..........................................**$15.00**

Additional sets, each.............................. **3.00**

When ordering, state if plans are to be reversed. Kindly mail remittance with order. Plans shipped within two hours on receipt of order.

**FLOOR PLAN**

## Design No. 240

Tʜɪs English type bungalow is 28 ft. across the front, 26 ft. across the back, and 34 ft. long. It is an artistic and comfy little home, so different from anything else; the exterior walls and roof are dipped shingles. A basement extends under entire house; the interior arrangement is most practical in every detail, no waste space anywhere and every convenience is provided.

Hot air heat is recommended.

Price of one complete set of Plans, Specifications and Material
List...........................................................**$15.00**
Additional sets, each.............................. **3.00**

When ordering, state if plans are to be reversed. Kindly mail remittance with order. Plans shipped within two hours on receipt of order.

Spanish Square Type. This house is 26x26, exclusive of sun room—a very practical and distinctive design. The brickwork from the base to window sills, with stucco above and wide eaves, produces a pleasing combination. The interior arrangement is most practical, the hall, living room, sun room and dining room, produce a beautiful effect. You will note that this plan has four chambers, all well arranged and proportioned, and all available space has been utilized. Every up-to-the-minute convenience has been provided. Hot water heat is recommended.

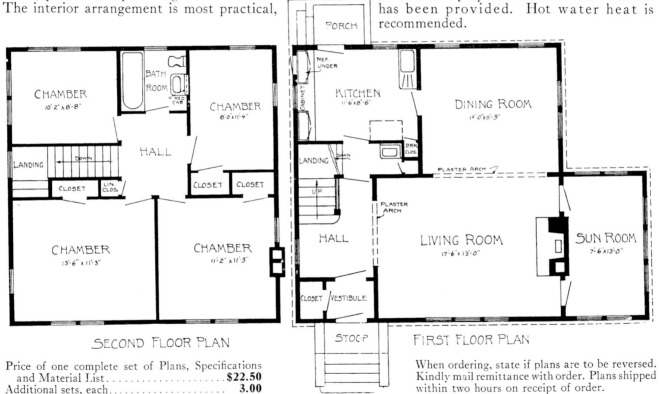

SECOND FLOOR PLAN

FIRST FLOOR PLAN

Price of one complete set of Plans, Specifications
  and Material List....................**$22.50**
Additional sets, each...................  **3.00**

When ordering, state if plans are to be reversed. Kindly mail remittance with order. Plans shipped within two hours on receipt of order.

80

Design No. 28

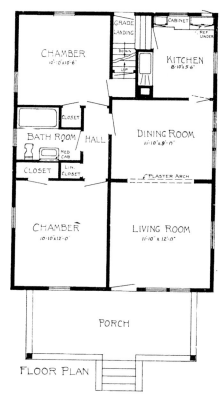

CHAMBER
10'-0"x10'-6"

GRADE
LANDING

CABINET

REF. UNDER

DOWN

UP

KITCHEN
8'-10"x9'-6"

CLOSET

BATH ROOM

HALL

MED. CAB.

CLOSET

LIN. CLOSET

DINING ROOM
11'-10"x9'-0"

PLASTER ARCH

CHAMBER
10'-10"x12'-0"

LIVING ROOM
11'-10" x 12'-0"

PORCH

FLOOR PLAN

Price of one complete set of Plans, Specifications and Material List. **$12.50**
Additional sets, each............ **3.00**
When ordering, state if plans are to be reversed. Kindly mail remittance with order. Plans shipped within two hours on receipt of order.

**Design No. 104**

THIS bungalow is 24x32. It is neat in appearance and economical to construct, and is of a design that is in heavy demand. It is of frame construction throughout. The interior is practical and convenient, and all of the floor space has been utilized. Basement under entire house, with grade entrance. Also a large attic. All modern conveniences provided.

Hot air heat can be used to advantage in this house.

FLOOR PLAN

## Design No. 102

THIS artistic bungalow is 24x26 and is the smallest house in this book. It is a design that will meet a long-felt want everywhere among people of modest means. It is a most economical house to construct, and yet has an artistic appearance as well as a most complete and practical interior arrangement commensurate with its outside dimensions. Basement under entire house.

The illustration does not show an additional window in kitchen; this is included in plans and blue prints to give better light.

Price of one complete set of Plans, Specifications and
    Material List...................................$10.00
Additional sets, each.............................. 3.00
When ordering, state if plans are to be reversed. Kindly mail remittance with order. Plans shipped within two hours on receipt of order.

**SECOND FLOOR PLAN**

CHAMBER
11'-0" x 9'-0"

LANDING

Down

Tub

CLOS.

HALL

CHAMBER
10'-9" x 14'-0"

BATH ROOM

W.C. LAV. Med. Cab.

CLOS. CLOS.

CHAMBER
16'-0" x 12'-0"

Ref Under

Cabinet

KITCHEN
11'-0" x 8'-6"

Sink

LAV. Br. Clos.

CLOS.

Down

GRADE LANDING

SUN ROOM
10'-9" x 9'-6"

UP

Plas. Arch

Cabinet

BREAKFAST NOOK

Plas Arch

LIVING ROOM
17'-9" x 13'-3"

DINING ROOM
11'-0" x 12'-6"

VESTIBULE

**FIRST FLOOR PLAN**

STOOP

Here is a delightful quaint Old English cottage type house, 30x28½. Simplicity of design is the keynote; its steep roof, nicely arranged windows, and front entrance with wrought iron railings make a very interesting horizontal effect. The house may be placed upon a 40 foot lot. It is planned to meet the requirements of the twentieth century citizen. The first floor is well arranged; the second floor contains three good sized bed rooms and a bath room, all opening into the hall in the center.

Price for one complete set of Plans, Specifications and Material List..................................$25.00

Additional sets, each............................ 3.00

When ordering, state if plans are to be reversed. Kindly mail remittance with order. Plans shipped within two hours on receipt of order.

Design No. 46

SECOND FLOOR PLAN

FIRST FLOOR PLAN

## Design No. 154

In this Semi-Bungalow, 24x26, there is all the compactness of a bungalow combined with the privacy afforded by a second story.

All possible monotony of line has been avoided by the dormer which breaks the otherwise straight lines of the roof, and gives an airy chamber in the second floor. Further variation in design has been accomplished by another slope to the porch roof, making a fair sized porch which may be screened. Note the large living room, grade landing at side, combination stairway from living room and kitchen, and a particularly convenient and compact arrangement of second floor.

Price of one complete set of Plans, Specifications and Material List......**$17.50**
Additional sets, each.............. **3.00**
When ordering, state if plans are to be reversed. Kindly mail remittance with order. Plans shipped within two hours on receipt of order.

## Design No. 136

Design No. 136. Spanish Bungalow, 26x34 in size. Finished in rough stucco, with variegated composition roof and various colors of brick to bring out an odd effect. A vestibule leads into the living room, and we have both dining room and living room in the front of the house. Living room has fireplace in it. This bungalow may be built on a narrow lot.

There is a full basement underneath and hot water or hot air heat can be installed.

Price of one complete set of Plans, Specifications and
    Material List . . . . . . . . . . . . . . . . . . . . . . . . . . . . . . . . . **$15.00**
Additional sets, each . . . . . . . . . . . . . . . . . . . . . . . . . . . . **3.00**
When ordering, state if plans are to be reversed. Kindly mail remittance with order. Plans shipped within two hours on receipt of order.

**S**EMI-BUNGALOW. This semi-bungalow, 26½x30, well deserves its popularity. The first feature to impress the visitor is the spacious porch—a boon to the apartment dweller who in the summer time has felt the need of just such a haven. Entering the house, one notices an artistic arch opening leading from the large living room to the dining room and another leading to the stairway. The entire house has been planned with an eye to comfort as well as attractiveness. The interior plans include many up-to-the-minute conveniences.

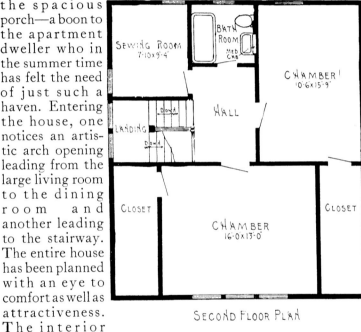

SECOND FLOOR PLAN

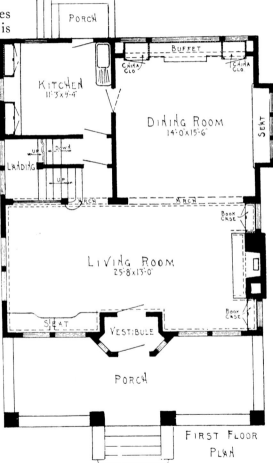

FIRST FLOOR PLAN

Price of one complete set of Plans, Specifications and Material List... .............................................**$20.00**
Additional sets, each.......................................  3.00

When ordering, state if plans are to be reversed.  Kindly mail remittance with order.  Plans shipped within two hours on receipt of order.

Design No. 257

KITCHEN
9'-0 x

GRADE
LANDING

CABINET

BATH
ROOM

CLOS

CHAMBER
9'8 x 12'6

HALL

DINING ROOM
13'-0 x 11'-0

CHAMBER
12'-9 x 11'-0

PLASTER ARCH

CLOS | CLOSET

LIVING ROOM
15'-9 x 13'-0

PLASTER ARCH

SUN ROOM
OR CHAMBER
9'-0 x 13'-6

VESTIBULE

FIRST FLOOR
PLAN

STOOP

Price of one complete set of Plans,
Specifications and Material List.**$17.50**
Additional sets, each............ **3.00**
When ordering, state if plans are to be reversed. Kindly mail remittance with
order. Plans shipped within two hours
on receipt of order.

**Design No. 100**

Spanish Bungalow. This new
Spanish Bungalow is 26x42.
It is very unique and beautiful, a
decided departure from the other
bungalow types. The exterior is
ivory stucco, with a red shingled
roof. The interior is most attractive and practical, and every convenience is provided. The room
designated as sun room or chamber, can be made to serve either
purpose as requirements may be.

Basement extends under entire
house, with grade door at rear.

90

FLOOR PLAN

## Design No. 108

Bungalow. This unusual thatched-roof bungalow is 30x30. It has a brick base, with stucco above and asphalt shingles on roof.

The interior is also out of the ordinary, having the center hall with living and dining rooms on either side and plaster Gothic arches between. The remaining rooms are also very conveniently arranged.

Basement under entire house with grade entry at side.

Hot water or hot air heat can be used.

Price of one complete set of Plans, Specifications and
    Material List. . . . . . . . . . . . . . . . . . . . . . . . . . . . . . . . . .**$15.00**
Additional sets, each. . . . . . . . . . . . . . . . . . . . . . . . . . . . **3.00**
When ordering, state if plans are to be reversed. Kindly mail remittance with order. Plans shipped within two hours on receipt of order.

DUTCH COLONIAL. This house is 30x24, exclusive of sun room. The exterior is true to the Dutch Colonial architecture and presents a most satisfying appearance. The brick foundation, wide rustic siding and green shingles on roof produce a very attractive combination.

The interior, with center hall and stairway, with arches leading to living room and dining room, give an appearance of greatness. All of the other arrangements are as perfect in every way as can be made throughout. Hot water heat is recommended for a house of this type-

SECOND FLOOR PLAN

FIRST FLOOR PLAN

Price of one complete set of Plans, Specifications and
    Material List.................................$25.00
Additional sets, each..............................  3.00

When ordering, state if plans are to be reversed. Kindly mail remittance with order. Plans shipped within two hours on receipt of order.

Design No. 8

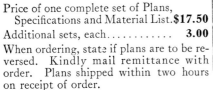

FLOOR PLAN

**Design No. 140**

Price of one complete set of Plans,
Specifications and Material List.**$17.50**
Additional sets, each............ **3.00**
When ordering, state if plans are to be reversed. Kindly mail remittance with
order. Plans shipped within two hours
on receipt of order.

DESIGN No. 140. Spanish Bungalow type, 31x32, extreme dimensions, exclusive of breakfast nook. Here is a Spanish effect which we predict will be one of our most popular designs. Neat and trim in appearance, and markedly horizontal lines, it suggests a touch of the Italian Villa. The dark doorway with its arch above, the windows not too large and the ground floor terrace with iron railing, lend to this design the appearance sought for in the Italian or Spanish Bungalow.

The interior arrangement deserves special mention, as it is a decided departure from any other plans. Here is a fine large living room with fireplace, and the dining room directly back, gives an air of spaciousness. Kitchen is on one side of the dining room, and on the left is the hall leading to the two chambers and bath. A stairway leads to a room on the second floor which may be finished off, if desired. If necessary, the breakfast nook can be left off to fit the house to a narrower lot.

FLOOR PLAN

## Design No. 130

A STRIKING bungalow of the Spanish type, 26 feet by 32 feet in size. It is finished in ivory stucco and red asphalt shingles. A red tile roof would give a nicer Spanish feeling to the exterior, but this makes it somewhat more expensive. The doorway is characteristic of the Spanish or Italian type. The house has a grade entrance at the side into the kitchen. The floor plan is nicely arranged, with the fireplace in the living room. For the money expended for this bungalow, nothing better could be devised.

Price of one complete set of Plans, Specifications and
  Material List.................................**$15.00**
Additional sets, each............................ **3.00**
When ordering, state if plans are to be reversed. Kindly mail remittance with order. Plans shipped within two hours on receipt of order.

**F**RAME SQUARE TYPE HOUSE. This attractive 26x28 house is always staple, and is economical and easy to construct.

Siding and stained shingles are used on the exterior wall, with red stained shingles on roof.

The well-planned interior will comfortably accommodate a large family.

The basement is fully equipped.

Hot water heat is recommended.

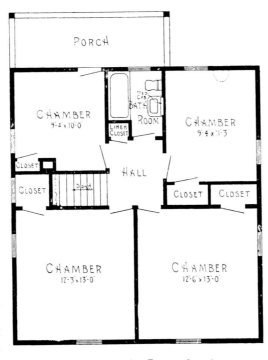

SECOND FLOOR PLAN

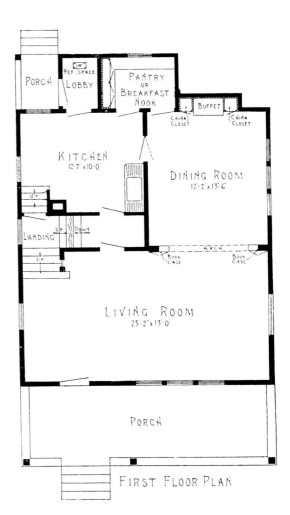

FIRST FLOOR PLAN

Price for one complete set of Plans, Specifications and Material List . . . . . . . . . . . . . . . . . . . . . . . . . . . . . . . . . . . . . . . . . . **$20.00**

Additional sets, each . . . . . . . . . . . . . . . . . . . . . . . . . . . . . . . **3.00**

When ordering, state if plans are to be reversed. Kindly mail remittance with order. Plans shipped within two hours on receipt of order.

Design No. 9

SECOND FLOOR PLAN

FIRST FLOOR PLAN

## Design No. 142

THIS practical and popular semibungalow, 22x26 in size, is of entirely frame construction, with concrete block foundation and basement under entire house. Although the exterior dimensions are small, the house has all the features of a larger one, such as large living room, sun room, porch, combination stairway, large closets, and an excellent room arrangement which creates a fine and spacious interior effect.

All conveniences are provided; hot air or hot water may be used for heating.

Price of one complete set of Plans, Specifications and Material List.........**$17.50**
Additional sets, each............... **3.00**
When ordering, state if plans are to be reversed. Kindly mail remittance with order. Plans shipped within two hours on receipt of order.

SECOND FLOOR PLAN

FIRST FLOOR PLAN

## Design No. 120

Semi-Bungalow, 22x26, of frame construction throughout. The first floor, with large living room, dining room, kitchen, with combination stairway from both living room and kitchen, also stairway to side grade entry and basement, are practical and convenient features. The second floor is well planned, with ample closets from both chambers and hall.

Price of one complete set of Plans, Specifications and Material List.... **$15.00**
Additional sets, each............ **3.00**
When ordering, state if plans are to be reversed. Kindly mail remittance with order. Plans shipped within two hours on receipt of order.

S EMI-BUNGALOW. This very attractive semi-bungalow, 24½x27, is artistic and beautiful and meets with approval everywhere. Even a casual examination of the plans will disclose reasons for this popularity. Would that you could examine the actual house with its sun room, large living room and dining room, with French doors and large arched opening between them. To describe such an interior is so much less impressive than to show it to you and let it speak for itself.

The second floor is well arranged and has ample closet room. Every available inch of space in this house has been utilized to the best advantage.

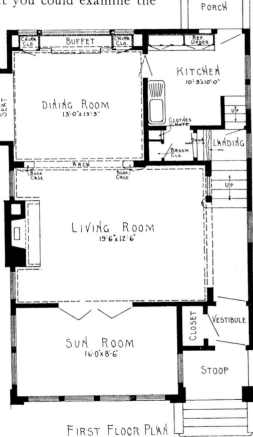

SECOND FLOOR PLAN

FIRST FLOOR PLAN

Price of one complete set of Plans, Specifications and Material List.**$25.00**
Additional sets, each . . . . . . . . . . . . . . . . . . . . . . . . . . . . . . . . . . . . . . . **3.00**
When ordering, state if plans are to be reversed. Kindly mail remittance with order. Plans shipped within two hours on receipt of order.

Design No. 151

**Design No. 114**

$B$UNGALOW. This cozy bungalow is 26x32 over all. For a man of modest means, this is an ideal home.

The interior includes a living room, kitchen, two chambers, sun room, dinette and bath room, grade entry to basement and ample closets. All conveniences are provided and the home is complete in every detail.

Stucco or siding may be used on outside walls. Hot air can be used to advantage in this bungalow.

Price of one complete set of Plans, Specifications and Material List..............................................**$12.50**
Additional sets, each...............................**3.00**
When ordering, state if plans are to be reversed. Kindly mail remittance with order. Plans shipped within two hours on receipt of order.

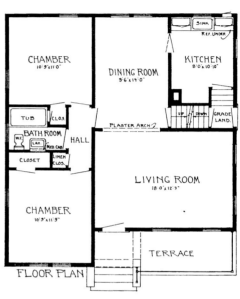

CHAMBER
10'5"x11'0"

DINING ROOM
9'6"x17'0"

KITCHEN
8'0"x10'10"

SINK
REF.UNDER

TUB  CLOS.

BATH ROOM

W.C.  LAV.  MED.CAB

HALL

PLASTER ARCH 2

UP  DOWN

GRADE
LAND.

CLOSET  LINEN
CLOS.

CHAMBER
10'5"x11'9"

LIVING ROOM
18'0"x12'3"

TERRACE

FLOOR PLAN

## Design No. 250

Tʜɪs Spanish bungalow is 30x32 extreme dimensions; it is an architectural gem of a home, as the picture can better reveal than words. The outside walls are stucco as all Spanish houses have to be, the roof is variegated asphalt shingles. A more ideal interior arrangement is impossible to devise, considering size of house. A space for everything and all conveniences provided; basement under entire house, also attic with stairs.

Hot air heat is recommended.

Price of one complete set of Plans, Specifications and Material
  List...........................................**$15.00**
Additional sets, each.............................. **3.00**
When ordering, state if plans are to be reversed.  Kindly mail remittance with order.  Plans shipped within two hours on receipt of order.

**S**QUARE **T**YPE. This house is 24x26, exclusive of porch and sun room, is of frame construction and a very staple, practical house in every way. This house embodies both the porch and sun room features which are so much desired by many. The interior arrangement is convenient and practical and every inch of floor area has been utilized to the best advantage. A most satisfactory house in every respect.

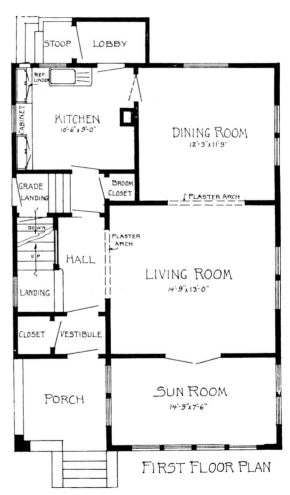

SECOND FLOOR PLAN

FIRST FLOOR PLAN

Price of one complete set of Plans, Specifications and Material List.**$20.00**
Additional sets, each........................................ **3.00**
When ordering, state if plans are to be reversed. Kindly mail remittance with order. Plans shipped within two hours on receipt of order.

104

Design No. 22

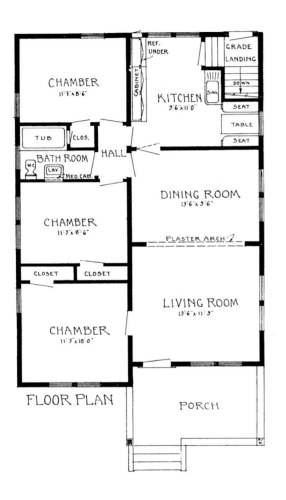

FLOOR PLAN

THIS bungalow is 26 ft. wide and 36 ft. extreme length. The house is designed for the man of small means and large family. The design is plain, so made to hold down the cost of construction and less expensive for upkeep; although plain it has a certain richness and comfiness and solidity about it that is hard to describe and owner can feel proud of its possession. A cement water table extends around entire house, with stucco walls and asphalt roof. The interior arrangement is as perfect as human ingenuity can make it, considering size of house. Three chambers with ample closets, bath, kitchen with breakfast nook, good size living room and dining room, grade landing to basement, which extends under entire house, makes a most desirable home at small cost. Fir inside trim with ivory and enamel finish makes a cheerful interior; oak floors in living and dining rooms and maple floors in remainder of house.

Hot air heat is recommended for heating this house, as it saves radiator space.

Price of one complete set of Plans, Specifications and Material List.**$15.00**
Additional sets, each. . . . . . . . . . . . . . . . . . . . . . . . . . . . . . . . . . . . **3.00**

When ordering, state if plans are to be reversed. Kindly mail remittance with order. Plans shipped within two hours on receipt of order.

106

Design No. 224

**S**EMI-BUNGALOW. This attractive semi-bungalow is 24½x28. This particular design enjoys well-merited popularity

Note especially the many exceptional interior features—the breakfast nook, combination stairway, balcony for airing bed clothes, ample closet room. The house is complete and convenient in every respect and, considering its dimensions, the rooms are of good size and well arranged.

This is a house which any family will soon convert into a comfortable home. One can get more satisfaction out of owning it than he could possibly get out of thousands of dollars worth of cancelled rent checks.

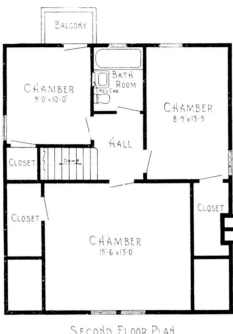

SECOND FLOOR PLAN

FIRST FLOOR PLAN

Price of one complete set of Plans, Specifications and Material List. **$20.00**
Additional sets, each..........................................  **3.00**

When ordering, state if plans are to be reversed. Kindly mail remittance with order. Plans shipped within two hours on receipt of order.

Design No. 5

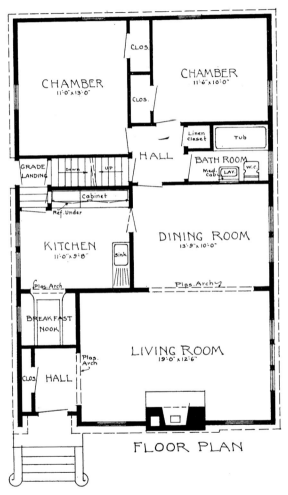

**FLOOR PLAN**

Within the plan, the following room labels appear:

CLOS.

CHAMBER
11'-0"x13'-0"

CHAMBER
11'-6"x10'-0"

CLOS.

Linen closet

Tub

HALL

BATH ROOM

GRADE LANDING

Down

Up

Med. cab.

LAV.

W.C.

Cabinet

Ref. Under

KITCHEN
11'-0"x9'-8"

Sink

DINING ROOM
13'-9"x10'-0"

Plas. Arch

Plas. Arch

BREAKFAST NOOK

LIVING ROOM
19'-0"x12'-6"

Plas. Arch

CLOS

HALL

A VERY unique bungalow, 26x40 in size. Most everyone, in deciding to build, wants a house which is different from the ordinary. This English type semi-bungalow gives an opportunity to deviate from the common to the elite, and secure a very artistic result. The craggy broken ashlar is limestone, blue and yellow, laid flatwise, with gray stucco and variegated asphalt shingles on the roof. The location of the chimney in front makes it an important element in the design, and gives the fireplace an unusual position in the living room.

The interior is well arranged and practical. Note the front hall with coat closet, large living room, 19'x12'6". Then there is a cheerful, fair sized dining room, and kitchen with breakfast nook. There is a refrigerator placed for icing from hallway, with grade entrance at side leading to kitchen and to basement. There is plenty of space for kitchen cabinet and a convenient position for the sink and stove; this kitchen arrangement is planned to save steps for the housewife. Two commodious chambers with closets are connected into the center hall, from which you can enter the bath room. A stairway to the second floor leads up from this center hall; two rooms here may be finished off, if desired, and still leave large space for storage purposes.

Oak, fir, or birch may be used for interior finish; and may be finished in any manner, as the specifications are drawn so as to give the owner his own choice.

Price for one complete set of Plans, Specifications and Material List . . . . . . . . . . . . . . . . . . . . . . . . . . . . . . . . . . . . . . . . . . . . . . . . . . . **$17.50**
Additional sets, each . . . . . . . . . . . . . . . . . . . . . . . . . . . . . . . . . . . . . . . **3.00**

When ordering, state if plans are to be reversed. Kindly mail remittance with order. Plans shipped within two hours on receipt of order.

Design No. 52

THIS bungalow is 26x38 and is a California style design. The exterior is very striking and unique, yet simple in construction. An eight-inch smooth troweled water table extends around entire house, with stucco above to belt course, and shingles in the gables. The roof is covered with shingles. The interior, as will be noticed, provides for three chambers, which is a rare accomplishment in bungalow construction, considering the small ground area this house occupies. The living room with large fireplace, having bookcases on each side, arch between living room and dining room, contribute to produce an effective interior. Beamed ceiling and built-in features may be eliminated. The center hall connects two chambers, bath room, dining room and kitchen, which is an excellent feature. The kitchen is provided with cabinet having refrigerator space for outside icing, breakfast nook, with table and seats, and door to grade landing, leading to basement and outside. The finish in living room and dining room may be oak or fir, old English finish, or birch, stained mahogany. The balance of house may be birch or fir, old ivory finish, with mahogany stained doors. Basement under entire house; provided with laundry tubs and dust proof coal bin.

Hot water heat is recommended, also modern plumbing fixtures throughout.

Price of one complete set of Plans, Specifications and Material List..........................................**$17.50**
Additional sets, each........................................ **3.00**

When ordering, state if plans are to be reversed. Kindly mail remittance with order. Plans shipped within two hours on receipt of order.

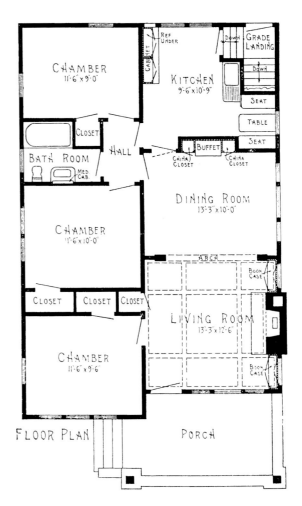

Design No. 49

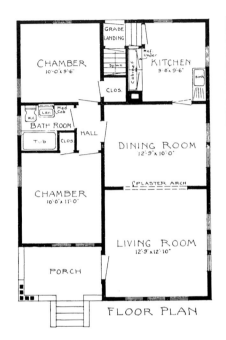

FLOOR PLAN

**Design No. 122**

DESIGN No. 122. Frame bungalow, size 24x34, extreme dimensions, including front porch. It has sufficient artistic lines to make it different from the general type of bungalows. Its rectangular shape permits a spacious and excellent arrangement of rooms. It can be built on a 35 foot lot if necessary. The blue prints call for all modern conveniences; this is a comfortable little bungalow which will meet the requirements of most families.

Price for one complete set of Plans, Specifications and Material List . . . . . . . . . . . . . . . . . . . . . . . . . . . . . . . . . . . . . .**$12.50**
Additional sets, each . . . . . . . . . . . . . . . . . . . . . . . . . . . . **3.00**

When ordering, state if plans are to be reversed. Kindly mail remittance with order. Plans shipped within two hours on receipt of order.

FLOOR PLAN

**Design No. 97**

J APANESE effect Bungalow. The size is 26x40, a very unique and beautiful design; the broken yellow stone around the base and in the chimney, stucco walls and variegated dipped shingles on roof, produce a charming effect. A careful study of floor plan will reveal a most perfect arrangement, everything has been provided; basement under entire house.

Hot water or hot air for heating; either can be used.

Price of one complete set of Plans, Specifications and Material List . . . . . . . . . . . . . . . . . . . . . . . . . . . . . . . . . . . . . . . . . . . . .**$17.50**
Additional sets, each . . . . . . . . . . . . . . . . . . . . . . . . . . . . . . **3.00**

When ordering, state if plans are to be reversed. Kindly mail remittance with order. Plans shipped within two hours on receipt of order.

THIS semi-bungalow is 26x40. Its exterior appearance has a feeling of stability as well as of beauty. If the plans are strictly carried out, they will produce a most satisfactory home. Brick and stucco are used on the exterior walls, and asphalt shingles on the roof. There is a well arranged and convenient floor plan, similar in some respects to Design No. 52. We have the front hall with coat closet; a plaster arch leading to the large light living room, fireplace in living room and Gothic arch leading into dining room. When properly finished and decorated it will produce a very striking appearance.

There is a side grade entry at the left to kitchen and basement. Kitchen has breakfast nook, cabinet provided with drawers, bins, closets and shelves, and a refrigerator space for icing from hall. The sink is conveniently placed; and the arrangement is so planned as to make it most convenient for the housewife or maid.

The chambers are commodious and the windows are so placed that beds and dressers may be placed in various positions. There is good closet space. Note that the bedrooms have cross drafts, so much to be desired in warm weather. All rooms lead into the center hall from which you can enter the bathroom. A stairway to attic is provided in which two or three rooms may be finished off, if desired. The interior woodwork should be of oak, birch or fir, finished in Old English, Mahogany, Ivory, Walnut or natural.

The basement extends under entire house and is provided with laundry tubs, vegetable cellar and coal bin.

Either hot water or hot air may be used for heating this home.

Price for one complete set of Plans, Specifications and Material List. **$17.50**
Additional sets, each.............................................. **3.00**
When ordering, state if plans are to be reversed. Kindly mail remittance with order. Plans shipped within two hours on receipt of order.

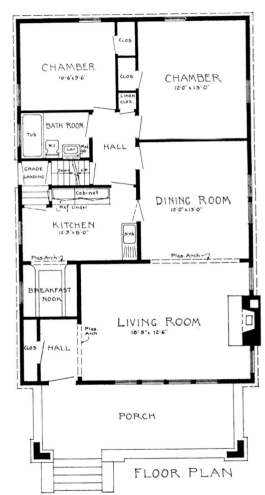

Design No. 50

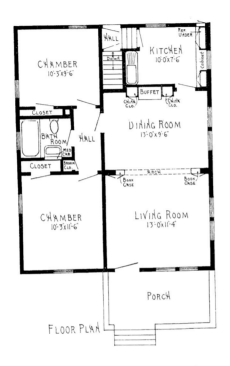

FLOOR PLAN

**Design No. 207**

THIS bungalow is 24x30 feet. The simplicity of the exterior construction is the keynote of this house and still it embodies correct architectural lines. Considering the floor area, everything possible has been accomplished as regards the interior arrangement, which is provided with five rooms and bath, having sufficient closet room and basement stair space. This is a snug little home for the family that has decided to drop the landlord from the pay-roll. It is neat, compact and attractive.

Price of one complete set of Plans, Specifications and Material List........................................**$12.50**
Additional sets, each.............................**3.00**
When ordering, state if plans are to be reversed. Kindly mail remittance with order. Plans shipped within two hours on receipt of order.

FLOOR PLAN

## Design No. 381

BUNGALOW, 24x32. The exterior is simple in construction and still retains good architectural lines. Stucco is used to the window sills, and stained shingles above. Considering the ground area the interior is extraordinarily well arranged and fair sized rooms have been obtained. It also embodies features found in larger houses, such as fireplace, Gothic bookcase arch and buffet and china closets which present a homey appearance. A small family will get a great deal of comfort out of this compact little house.

Price of one complete set of Plans, Specifications and Material List........................................................**$12.50**
Additional sets, each.............................. **3.00**
When ordering, state if plans are to be reversed. Kindly mail remittance with order. Plans shipped within two hours on receipt of order.

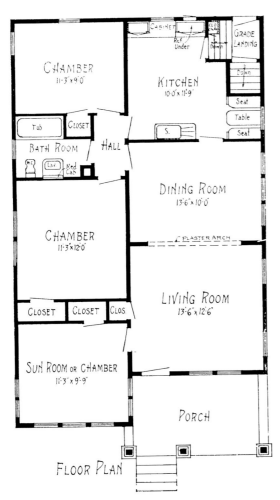

CHAMBER
11·3"x9·0"

KITCHEN
10·0"x11·9"

CABINET

Ref Under

CLO. SEAT

GRADE LANDING

Down

Seat

Table

Seat

Tub

CLOSET

BATH ROOM

HALL

S.

WC

Lav.

Med Cab

DINING ROOM
13·6"x10·0"

CHAMBER
11·3"x12·0"

CL. PLASTER ARCH

CLOSET

CLOSET

CLOS.

LIVING ROOM
13·6"x12·6"

SUN ROOM OR CHAMBER
11·3"x9·9"

PORCH

FLOOR PLAN

This bungalow, 26x41, has a concrete block foundation under the entire house. The exterior walls are of narrow siding and shingles in gable, with green stained shingles on roof. The interior is exceptionally well planned, as well as convenient. It is a plan which can be adjusted to meet the requirements of a fairly large family, by using the room, designated as sun room, as a chamber. On the other hand, if only two chambers are desired, this room is admirably situated for a sun room. If it is used, you can eliminate the door and have either arch opening or French doors. Besides this sun room, you can have a cozy porch, screened in summer and sashed in winter. The living room and dining room are of good size with plaster arch between them. The kitchen has a breakfast nook, kitchen cabinet with refrigerator space for outside icing, also grade entry to basement.

The center hall, leading to kitchen, chambers, bath room and dining room is another admirable feature in this plan.

The woodwork may be fir, birch or oak, finished walnut, old ivory, mahogany, or old English. Chambers should be white enamel with doors stained mahogany.

The basement has laundry tubs, vegetable room and coal bin.

Hot water or hot air heat may be used.

Price of one complete set of Plans, Specifications and Material List.**$17.50**
Additional sets, each . . . . . . . . . . . . . . . . . . . . . . . . . . . . . . . . . . . . . . . . . . . **3.00**
When ordering, state if plans are to be reversed. Kindly mail remittance with order. Plans shipped within two hours on receipt of order.

Design No. 42

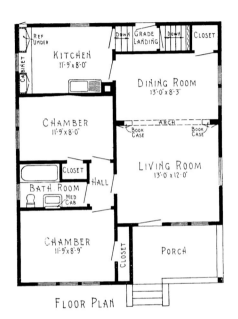

FLOOR PLAN

**Design No. 78**

THIS bungalow is 26x34 feet, inclusive of porch, and is unique in design and economical in construction. Siding is used from water table to cornice. The interior has been very competently arranged, having living room, with arch leading to dining room, two chambers, bath room and kitchen.

Price of one complete set of Plans, Specifications and Material List............................................**$15.00**
Additional sets, each............................... **3.00**
When ordering, state if plans are to be reversed. Kindly mail remittance with order. Plans shipped within two hours on receipt of order.

**Design No. 77**

Tᴴɪꜱ bungalow is 24x32, the front portion being 28 feet wide. The exterior is very attractive and immediately commands attention. A 27-inch smooth troweled water table extends around entire house with narrow siding above and shingles in the gables. The interior is beautiful and also very well arranged. The center hall connects dining room, both chambers and bath room. The kitchen is provided with cabinet, having refrigerator space for outside icing, also door to grade landing leading to basement and outside.

Price of one complete set of Plans, Specifications and Material
List..................................................**$15.00**
Additional sets, each................................. **3.00**
When ordering, state if plans are to be reversed. Kindly mail remittance with order. Plans shipped within two hours on receipt of order.

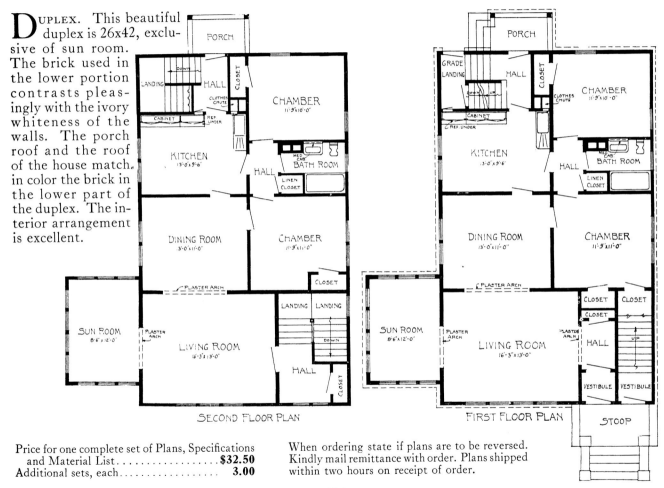

**D**UPLEX. This beautiful duplex is 26x42, exclusive of sun room. The brick used in the lower portion contrasts pleasingly with the ivory whiteness of the walls. The porch roof and the roof of the house match in color the brick in the lower part of the duplex. The interior arrangement is excellent.

PORCH

LANDING

DOWN

HALL

CLOSET

CLOTHES CHUTE

CHAMBER
11'-9"x10'-0"

CABINET

REF. UNDER

KITCHEN
13'-0"x9'-6"

MED. CAB.

BATH ROOM

HALL

LINEN CLOSET

DINING ROOM
13'-0"x11'-0"

CHAMBER
11'-9"x11'-0"

PLASTER ARCH

CLOSET

SUN ROOM
8'-6"x12'-0"

PLASTER ARCH

LANDING  LANDING

LIVING ROOM
16'-3"x13'-0"

DOWN

HALL

CLOSET

SECOND FLOOR PLAN

PORCH

GRADE LANDING

HALL

CLOSET

DOWN  UP

CLOTHES CHUTE

CHAMBER
11'-9"x10'-0"

CABINET

REF. UNDER

KITCHEN
13'-0"x9'-6"

MED. CAB.

BATH ROOM

HALL

LINEN CLOSET

DINING ROOM
13'-0"x11'-0"

CHAMBER
11'-9"x11'-0"

PLASTER ARCH

CLOSET  CLOSET

CLOSET

SUN ROOM
8'-6"x12'-0"

PLASTER ARCH

LIVING ROOM
16'-3"x13'-0"

PLASTER ARCH

HALL

UP

VESTIBULE  VESTIBULE

FIRST FLOOR PLAN

STOOP

Price for one complete set of Plans, Specifications
and Material List................$32.50
Additional sets, each................ 3.00

When ordering state if plans are to be reversed.
Kindly mail remittance with order. Plans shipped
within two hours on receipt of order.

124

Design No. 38

**D**UPLEX. This house is 28x48. One has to look closely to see that it is a duplex. Note the attractive living room on each floor with the fireplace and a bookcase on each side. This living room, a cozy fire on the hearth, a good book, a few cigars—what more could one ask on a winter's evening?

The builder of this home will have the advantage of receiving a steady income from the portion of it which he rents. This is a style of duplex which can easily be kept rented at a profitable rental.

Price of one complete set of Plans, Specifications and Material List.... **$35.00**
Additional sets, each **3.00**
When ordering, state if plans are to be reversed. Kindly mail remittance with order. Plans shipped within two hours on receipt of order.

SECOND FLOOR PLAN

FIRST FLOOR PLAN

126

Design No. 32

**Design No. 191**

FLOOR PLAN

Within the floor plan:
CHAMBER 11'-0"x8'-9"
HALL
KITCHEN 10'-8"x8'-3"
CLOSET
BROOM CLO.
BUFFET
BATH ROOM
MED. CAB.
HALL
DINING ROOM 13'-9"x9'-0"
CLOSET
BOOK CASE
ARCH
BOOK CASE
CHAMBER 11'-0"x12'-0"
LIVING ROOM 13'-9"x12'-0"
PORCH
SUN ROOM 9'-6"x7'-6"

This bungalow is 26x31 feet, exclusive of sun room. The exterior is all that the word nifty implies. The sun room effect in front of this bungalow adds a tone of superiority. The interior plan is perfect, its arrangement being very practical and strictly up-to-date, provision having been made for all necessary features. There is a basement under the entire house and modern conveniences are provided therein.

Hot water or hot air may be used for heating.

Price of one complete set of Plans, Specifications and Material List..........................................**$15.00**
Additional sets, each............................. **3.00**
When ordering, state if plans are to be reversed. Kindly mail remittance with order. Plans shipped within two hours on receipt of order.